Lean Productivity and Efficiency

Book 3 – Beyond Success Series

by

Mary Čolak

Published in 2023 by Discourse Books, Victoria, BC, Canada

www.marycolak.com

Cover design by impact studios

Library and Archives Canada Cataloguing in Publication

Lean productivity and efficiency: Beyond success / Mary Čolak

Includes bibliographical footnotes.

Paperback: ISBN: 978-1-7778086-5-5

Electronic book: ISBN 978-1-777-8086-6-2

1. Business & Economics / Operations Management

2. Business & Economics / Productivity

3. Self-help / Personal Growth / Success

****

*Being productive means having more time
to do the things you love.*

****

Coming Soon

Beyond Success Series

Communicating for Results

Getting a Handle on Records

Other books in this series:

Considerations in Making Money (Book 1)

Acquiring Time (Book 2)

Lean Productivity and Efficiency

Book 3 – Beyond Success Series

Contents

Introduction

Productivity Primer

Efficiency Primer

Lean Primer

DEFINE

Influential Leaders Enable Productive Organizations 19

A3 Problem-solving 21

The Problem 26

What is Value-Add and How Does it Impact
Efficiency? 30

The Power of Why 34

Distinguishing Between Needs and Requirements .. 37

Project Charter – Why Do We Need One, Anyway? .. 42

Preventing Projects from Going Sideways 45

Changing Behavior by Changing Situations 48

Resistance is Futile 51

Brainstorming—Not for Everyone 54

Business Value in a Post-Pandemic World 57

MEASURE

Peak Performers: Not Always Good for Business 61

Leaning for Success.. 64

In God we Trust; for Everything Else, There's Data. 68

Mapping the Inefficient Subprocess........................ 71

Tradition and Productivity 76

Leveraging the Power of Stakeholders.................... 79

Almighty Surveys 83

Eliminate DOWNTIME to Re-ignite Your Business
Post Pandemic.. 86

ANALYZE

Characteristics of the Perfect Team........................ 92

Customer Service 96

Turning Efficiency into Power................................. 99

The Fast Track to Change 102

Managing Inventories 105

Perfecting Products Before or After Launch 107

Understanding What Causes Problems.................. 110

Service – Now!.. 116

Cutting Costs and Optimizing Spend in Small and
Mid-size Enterprises 119

The Root of Airport Delays & Flight Cancellations. 126

IMPROVE

Kaizen to the Rescue 133

Accelerating Project Success 136

The #1 Red Light: A Lack of Urgency.................... 140

The 5S Method.. 143

The People Problem 146

That's The Way We Do It Here 149

How Organizations Can Identify Areas for
Improvement 152

Secrets to Project Success 156

Top Ways to Improve Team Dynamics on a Project 158

Using Internal Resources to Implement Projects ... 162

Best Practices for Effective Implementation Plans . 165

The Productivity Mindset 169

Learning at Work 172

Motivating for Change 176

Dimensions of Change 179

Head, Heart, Hands – Do You Know What You're
Doing? 182

Reclaiming Knowledge Work's Lost Productivity ... 185

Good, Better, Best 189

Out with the Old, In with the New 191

CONTROL

Measures of Control 195

What Keeps Leaders Awake? 198

Taming Insomnia to Improve Productivity 202

Secret to Enabling a Paradigm Shift 205

Moving to a Quality Culture 208

Efficiency is in the Toolkit 212

Open Office – Productivity Enabler or Slasher? 215

Leaders Helping Staff with Productivity 218

Six Steps for Achieving Quality 221

Procedures Par Excellence 225

Efficiency Overload 228

Bridging the Gap between Training & Proficiency . 231

About the Author

Introduction

The words lean, productivity, and efficiency imply similar concepts, but each word's meaning differs. Let me start with efficiency.

Efficiency is about accomplishing tasks with the least effort, quickly achieving a goal with the fewest necessary resources—producing something quickly without wasting resources.

On the other hand, productivity is the rate at which one produces a product or service. It's the ratio of outputs to inputs—the units of output divided by the units of input. For example, how many hours (input) it takes to write a book (output) measures the writer's productivity.

Another related term is effectiveness, i.e., doing the right things. Thus, there is a correlation between effectiveness, efficiency, and productivity. If you are doing the right things (being effective) and using the necessary resources (being efficient), you will be productive (producing the maximum output in the least amount of time).

Lean brings together productivity, efficiency, and effectiveness. It focuses on reducing waste. When your processes are free of waste (e.g., wasted time, effort, money, materials, etc.), you have a Lean and efficient operation. Thus, Lean helps organizations save time and money (check out my books on time and money – *Beyond Success: Acquiring Time* and *Beyond Success: Considerations in Making Money*).

In addition, there is an inextricable link between being organized and efficient. One feeds the other. If you're disorganized, then you're not efficient. If you think your disorganization is not a big deal, think again. Not only are you preventing yourself from being as efficient as possible, but you are also preventing your colleagues from being efficient since they must wait on you to complete tasks where your input is essential.

There is no room for disorganization in businesses (or at home, for that matter). Being disorganized eats up time, and this means money. In addition, if your office is chaotic, it can cost your company its credibility. But it's never too late to develop good habits. Try the *10-Minute Rule* to get organized. Here's how it works.

At the end of each day, take 10 minutes to clear the clutter from only 10 percent of your office. For simplicity's sake, let's say your office is about 100 square feet, then you tackle only 10 square feet at a time. In 10 days, you've decluttered and made your workspace efficient.

This short book of essays relating to productivity and efficiency through a Lean lens will help you improve your productivity and efficiency by eliminating waste and streamlining business processes. The following three articles, Productivity Primer, Efficiency Primer, and Lean Primer, introduce terms applied in this book. I hope you will want to implement a Lean process in your office because it is a common-sense approach to work and life. By the end of the book, you will better understand how to be productive, efficient, and effective while also learning how to save time and resources by reducing waste.

Following the primer essays, I divided the book into five sections, each section relating to one of the five phases of Lean – defining, measuring, analyzing, improving, and controlling (DMAIC). The essays within each section highlight relevant ideas applicable to each Lean phase.

Productivity Primer

Clients and others often ask me in what areas of an organization productivity improvements can make the most positive impact. There is no one correct answer to this question, but here are some things to consider.

Productivity improvement is a broad field and can include looking at how to increase organizational capital for better innovation, the effects of government policy on an organization's productivity, corporate design and how design affects productivity, and how to use technology to improve an organization's competitiveness.

Where productivity improvement can positively impact an organization depends on what area of the organization is performing the most poorly. You can determine which site performs poorly by assessing each organizational area and deciding where outputs are weak. There are two ways to do this.

The first is using a task-level analysis to determine whether one could do the task more quickly. Let's say it takes an average of five days to initiate and approve a request to purchase and install a computer in your organization. Breaking this task down into its parts, you may discover that you could reduce this number to two days by eliminating redundancies and the number of people involved. Thus, you've just identified a task that could improve productivity (the ratio of outputs divided by inputs).

The second way to determine areas for productivity improvement is at a structural or big-picture level. The big-picture approach is top-down and looks at the business vision and strategy, the organization's culture, core business competencies, and management systems. Productivity improvement at the structural level is more challenging since its inputs, such as the organization's vision and culture, are more philosophical. But it wouldn't be impossible to determine how the vision and culture affect what staff are working on and how they are working on the vision.

So, where should you begin? Here are eight steps that an organization can take to identify where productivity improvements would make the most impact:

1. Conduct a diagnosis and needs assessment to identify the systems and processes contributing to poor productivity in the organization. Include critical issues impacting current productivity levels and what needs to be addressed to improve productivity in each area. For example, if strategic projects are usually not completed

on time or within budget, ask "why" several times until you drill down to the answer(s) as to why this is happening. This approach will provide the necessary information to address and correct the situation.

2. Based on the "what needs to be addressed" items discovered during diagnosis, prepare an action plan that details how you will improve productivity in problem areas, including alternatives for each action item. Continuing from our example, if you discover that one of the reasons for projects running behind schedule is a lack of staff, then a possible action item is to "hire more staff." Other reasons may include a lack of knowledgeable staff, or perhaps there are sufficient staff, but more project management training is required, etc.

3. Based on the action plan, select the appropriate action items for implementation.

4. Prepare an implementation plan outlining how to implement each action item, including how you will measure productivity improvement for each action item. For example, if your action item is to hire more staff in a particular department, indicate how many staff you will employ and/or by what date and/or how many staff you will train in a specific area, etc.

5. Implement the action items and manage the change by training all staff in new policies, processes, and procedures that reflect how the action items will improve productivity in the organization. Include measures of success for each implemented action item. This approach will ensure greater compliance and productivity improvement.

6. Audit the implemented action items at three, six, and nine-month intervals. Using established measures of success, determine if productivity has improved. If productivity could be better, review the item and tweak the process as necessary to gain more productivity.

7. Manage the change by conducting regular audits (usually annual) of each implemented action item to ensure that productivity is sustained or continues to improve.

8. Every one or two years, repeat the process in the same or other areas to gain continuous improvement across the entire organization.

By following the above steps, you will improve productivity in your organization in the areas that most need improvement and, therefore, where your organization will see the most positive impact. However, remember also to follow sound change management principles and implement regular training for all staff.

Training is crucial to create process improvements, especially since the organization's people are responsible for productivity. Including your staff in the process will make the difference between productivity and profit or non-productivity and bankruptcy. The image below summarizes my eight steps for productivity improvement.

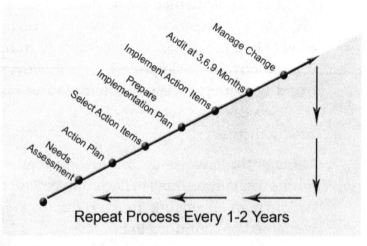

Repeat Process Every 1-2 Years

Efficiency Primer

Efficiency is the ability to complete a task or achieve a goal most effectively and optimally, using the least resources such as time, energy, or cost. It involves maximizing output while minimizing input. Efficiency is essential in various fields and industries, as it helps organizations and individuals streamline processes, reduce waste, increase productivity, and ultimately improve overall performance.

Becoming efficient can require effort and practice, but it is achievable with the right strategies and mindset. Efficiency is all about optimizing your time and resources to achieve better results in less time. One way to become more efficient is by prioritizing tasks and focusing on the ones with the highest impact on you and your organization (as the case may be). You can use your time better by identifying what's most critical and tackling those tasks first. Additionally, breaking down larger tasks into smaller, more manageable steps can help you stay motivated and progress more efficiently.

My book *Beyond Success: Acquiring Time* mentions that developing good time management skills and establishing routines can contribute to efficiency. Planning your day, setting goals, and creating a schedule can help you stay organized and allocate your time effectively. Avoiding multitasking and eliminating distractions can help you maintain focus and complete tasks more efficiently.

Efficiency is a habit that one can cultivate over time. Finding your best method might take trial and error, but with consistency and determination, you can become more efficient in your personal and professional endeavors. Here are my top four focus areas to operate more efficiently:

1. Workspace. A workspace that is free and clear of clutter enables efficiency and productivity. Here are some things to focus on in your workspace. Is the paper on your desk related only to the project on which you are currently working? Is your desk placed in such a way as to minimize distraction? Is your telephone set on the correct side of your desk (on the right if you're left-handed, on the left if you're right-handed)? I'm talking about landlines here, but this placement also works for mobile phones. Is your computer in an ergonomically correct position? What is the condition of your chair? Is there "space" in your office? Overall, is your office aesthetically pleasing that even your mother would be proud to visit?

2. Plan and prioritize. At the end of each day, plan and prioritize your work for the next day. You may even wish to do this for each week. By planning and prioritizing your day and sticking to your plan, you are less likely to get distracted by unimportant or non-urgent tasks and time wasters.

3. Self-management. Adopt habits that enable you to perform your best all the time. Learn to handle procrastination, personal disorganization, socializing, taking on too much work, and delegating. It's the little things compounded that derail efficiency.

4. External environment. Even when we have an efficient workspace, the best plans, and methods for prioritizing and self-managing, sometimes the work environment may pose distractions. To control the work environment so it doesn't impact your efficiency, learn to manage your telephone calls, email inbox, and drop-in visitors. Also, ensure meetings are well organized and use superb communication skills to handle even the most severe inefficiencies.

An efficient individual or organization can ultimately contain resources and costs in producing work. Thus, assuming efficient practices in all areas of client work means efficiency is just a short step to productivity and an increased bottom line. See my book, *Beyond*

Success: Acquiring Time, for tips on managing your workspace, plans, priorities, self, and the external environment.

The graphic below summarizes my four focus areas to help you operate efficiently and become more productive.

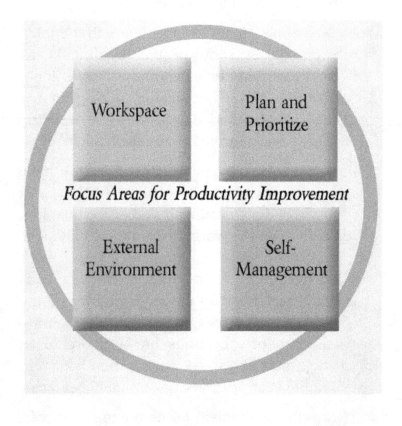

Workspace

Plan and Prioritize

Focus Areas for Productivity Improvement

External Environment

Self-Management

Lean Primer

At its core, Lean is about removing waste in processes to improve efficiency and productivity. Related to Lean is Six Sigma, which eliminates variability in the process. However, this book focuses on Lean; it does not delve into Six Sigma. Once you have a handle on Lean, it is relatively easy to take steps to reduce variability in processes—Lean and Six Sigma go hand-in-hand. By removing waste and variability, the process nears perfection. But since perfection is in the eye of the beholder, one never achieves it—one can only work toward its attainment.

Lean and Six Sigma projects follow a scientific approach in five phases. These phases are defining, measuring, analyzing, improving, and controlling (i.e., DMAIC), setting Lean and Six Sigma apart from traditional projects. In addition, DMAIC is not a linear model but overlaps as one works toward improving a process.

The define phase establishes the project focus and purpose for the project team. This phase includes the project charter, identifies and validates customers' needs and requirements, and creates a high-level picture of the process to focus the team's improvement efforts.

Defining the problem is the first step in the problem-solving process. It is a crucial stage where you clearly define the problem or opportunity you want to address. During this phase, you gain a deep understanding of the current situation, identify the root causes of the problem, and establish a clear goal for improvement. The step involves gathering data, facts, and stakeholder feedback through interviews, observations, surveys, and other means.

With solid information, you can define the scope and boundaries of the improvement project, along with measurable goals that align with the organization's overall objectives. The define phase sets the stage for the rest of the Lean process; it provides a foundation for problem-solving and improvement efforts. It helps ensure that everyone involved in the project understands the problem and the desired outcome, paving the way for effective implementation and success.

The second Lean phase concerns measurements and sees the team measuring the process through an established data collection plan. It is a critical step in the process. In the measure phase, the group gathers and analyzes data to gain insights into the current state of the process. Measuring the process performance at the outset establishes a baseline performance measure and understanding of its current performance. By measuring the process, you identify its strengths and weaknesses. Through collecting and analyzing quantitative and qualitative data, the Lean team can identify opportunities for improvement and set measurable goals for the subsequent phases of the Lean cycle.

In the analyze phase, the team investigates the data and observes the process, determining the root cause of problems to identify areas for process improvement. The analysis phase is the most important because it identifies the problem's root cause, crucial to successful Lean improvements. The team uses various tools and techniques in the analysis phase, such as process mapping, value stream mapping, root cause, and data analysis. The goal is to comprehensively understand the process's current state and identify specific areas or activities for improvement.

By analyzing data and information collected during the analyze phase, organizational teams can make informed decisions about which improvements to prioritize and implement in the subsequent stage of Lean (i.e., the improve and control phases). The analyze phase sets the foundation for data-driven process improvements.

The fourth phase, improvement, involves generating, selecting, and implementing solutions identified during the analyze phase. This phase is about changing existing processes and systems to achieve desired improvements. In this phase, teams experiment with different improvement ideas and solutions to see how they impact the process. They often conduct experiments on a small scale or in a controlled environment to minimize risks.

The main objective of the improvement phase is to implement changes that address the identified issues and achieve measurable results, such as reducing waste, enhancing efficiency, improving quality, or increasing customer satisfaction. This phase is critical since it is here that the organization can see pushback because people don't always adapt well to change. Even if the process is broken, many get comfortable and resist its improvement. Thus, the improvement phase requires gentle persuasion and a careful approach to implementation.

The improvement phase often involves collaboration and continuous communication among team members and process owners to ensure all stakeholders understand the improvements to implement them correctly. It is an iterative process where adjustments and refinements may be necessary to achieve the desired improvements.

The final phase of the Lean methodology cycle is the control phase. Organizations establish control mechanisms in this phase to sustain the improvements achieved during the analyze and improvement phases. The phase involves putting safeguards in place to ensure that the improved processes and systems operate effectively and efficiently over the long term. These safeguards include setting up monitoring and tracking systems to measure key performance indicators (KPIs) and regularly reviewing and analyzing the data to identify any deviations or potential issues. The control methods, such as a bar chart or a check sheet, could be statistical or straightforward. In addition, they outline the project and related problem response plans.

The control phase also involves implementing standardized work processes, creating visual management systems, and establishing regular audits to ensure compliance with the improved practices. Documenting the new processes and training employees to follow them consistently is crucial.

By maintaining control over the improved processes, organizations can prevent the reoccurrence of problems and sustain the improvements achieved through Lean methodology. Additionally, the control phase provides a feedback loop to continuously monitor improvement effectiveness and identify further enhancement or refinement opportunities.

Finally, the project team transfers the project to the process owner during the control phase.

DEFINE

Influential Leaders Enable Productive Organizations

As an effective leader, you know that specific competencies are necessary for your success on the job, things like building yourself as a whole person (emotionally, intellectually, spiritually, creatively), building winning teams, respecting others to earn their respect, communicating effectively, and inspiring others to build trust, just to name a few. You may also know that proven leadership methods aren't always the answer in every situation.

Enabling others to be as efficient, effective, and productive as possible is a crucial tenet of leadership. What is your staff working on? What systems, processes, and tools are they using to accomplish organizational goals? Are these systems, processes, and tools as efficient and effective as possible? These are questions that every leader should ask since the leaders' accountability is first to their staff to enable organizational productivity.

In addition to looking at overall organizational productivity, leaders need to talk to their staff and customers to understand the big picture because talking to other leaders or mentors will not inform you of your customers' thoughts. However, sometimes, neither will talking with your staff. So, instead, why not experience what your staff experiences? The show "Undercover Boss"[1] sets an excellent example for leaders. Putting yourself in your staff's shoes will teach you more about your organization's operations than you could ever learn from the company's policies and procedures manuals or strategic planning sessions.

What about mentors? Every leader needs two mentors–one half their age and the other twice their age. Currently, baby boomers are retiring or semi-retiring. The semi-retired remain in the job market in a part-time or entrepreneurial capacity. At the same time, Generation Y (those born between the late 1970s to the early 2000s) is in the job market. The joining of these two generations in the workplace saw a shift in information sharing. Not so long ago, leaders didn't need to think about tweets or texts; now they do. Seek mentors to help you bridge the gap between these two generations.

The bottom line is that leaders must continually evolve and practice their knowledge, values, skills, and behaviors. Taking elements of the tried and true methods such as those discussed above and modifying them to fit current situations enables good leaders to become influential leaders in productive organizations.

A3 Problem-solving

An A3 is an international paper, 11.7-by-16.5 inches, thus its name. It is twice the size of an A4 (8.27-by-11.69 inches) and half that of an A2 sheet. People commonly use an A3 for posters, diagrams, and large documents that require more space than a standard A4 sheet. Thus, A3 problem-solving involves a Lean approach to reporting issues and effectively presenting a situation—a story anyone can understand—on one page. Toyota developed this simple method, which focuses on documenting a problem, its current outcome, and proposed changes.

It is a visual tool for problem-solving because it presents all the main elements in a condensed space, allowing for on-the-spot review. It is a robust management process encouraging learning through a scientific problem-solving approach. It includes a description of the current conditions, goals, analysis, and an action plan for implementing solutions.

However, there is no standard format for presenting information using an A3. Instead, each A3 suits the situation. At the end of this article, I provide a detailed example that you can use and modify to suit your organization's situation.

However, regardless of format, an A3 answers the same basic questions:

1. What is the problem or issue?

2. Who owns the problem?

3. What is the root cause(s) of the problem?

4. What are some possible counter-measures?

5. How will you decide which counter-measures to propose?

6. How will you get agreement from everyone concerned?

7. What is your implementation plan – who, what, when, where, how?

8. How will you know if your counter-measures work?

9. What follow-up issues can you anticipate? What problems may occur during implementation?

10. How will you capture and share the learning?

Defining the problem is the key to using the A3 or any problem-solving approach. Too often, people start fixing symptoms of problems rather than the actual problem. This approach never achieves the desired long-term results.

In its simplest form, a problem is a barrier that prevents the organization from achieving its goals. A problem may also involve the design or performance of work. The gap between the existing and desired conditions is the problem. Achieving performance improvement occurs through understanding this gap.

There are a few reasons why the A3 is a popular tool for problem-solving and brainstorming.

1. Visual space. The large size of an A3 provides ample space to visualize and map ideas, diagrams, flowcharts, and other pictorial representations. This graphical approach can help teams better understand the problem and potentially identify new perspectives or solutions.

2. Collaboration. Since the size of an A3 is more extensive than traditional letter or legal-size sheets, it can enable group collaboration. Many individuals can contribute their thoughts visibly and tangibly on the sheet. This participation fosters effective communication, encourages diverse thinking, and promotes teamwork.

3. Structure. Depending on the situation, an A3 may already have predefined sections, which can guide the problem-solving exercise and ensure the team addresses the

critical aspects of the problem and devises a comprehensive solution.

4. Focus. The spaciousness of the A3 allows for precise and organized problem documentation. With dedicated spaces for specific aspects of a problem, it's easier to get a comprehensive overview, identify connections, and maintain focus throughout the process.

While A3 sheets are not the only tool available for problem-solving, they provide a tangible and visual means of capturing and organizing ideas and information, which can enhance the problem-solving process for individuals or teams.

The A3 is also useful for describing action items – a condensed project charter for each item covering one or two A3 sheets instead of multiple letter-sized typed pages. Once you start using the A3 format to assess your organization's problem areas, there's a good chance you will never return to traditional methods.

Project Name		Project Number

Project Charter Date	Version No.	Status	Prepared by

Project Initiator (Business Unit/Department) / Owner	Project Champion	Project Sponsor

Business Unit/Department (Owner)	Project Manager	Project Team Members

Problem Description—As reported by requestor	Problem Description—As reported by customers

Process Name

Process Start

Process End

Problem Description—As reported by employees	Problem Description—Other observations

Process – What is included

Process – What is excluded

Process Success Criteria (objectives and KPIs—SMART) - How will we measure success?
(Define KPI, associated objective/outcomes, baseline, and target measures)

Expected Gains—Tangible	Expected Gains—Intangible

Action Plan (include timeline and follow-up items)

Signature: Owner	Signature: Champion	Signature: Sponsor

Date	Date	Date

The Problem

Are you a player? Or are you a victim?

If you're a player, you choose to resolve problems. If you're a victim, you helplessly accept everything thrown your way. Whether one can say they have a problem is based solely on their perception of the situation.

Problems are not things. One cannot hold a problem. Instead, they are perceptions of things. We can see them as situations to avoid or as opportunities to embrace. Victims see problems as obstacles they cannot overcome and use language such as "should" or "not fair." Players, on the other hand, embrace problems as opportunities for change.

Every organization needs players. Players are the change agents without whom organizations die. Players help others in your organization interact, leading to shared beliefs and values and organizational goals and behaviors. Beliefs and values drive behaviors. For example, organizations with shared views of consistency, fairness, communication, and team involvement will display those beliefs through improved productivity, quality, group morale, and individual satisfaction. Organizations that do not have these behaviors need players to help change organizational beliefs.

If you're not a player in your organization, here are ten things you can do right now to move toward becoming a player. In turn, you will be helping yourself and your organization change for the better.

1. Buy part of the problem to be part of the solution. That is, see the problem for what it is – an opportunity to improve. Get involved in creating the solution.

2. Grow through adversity. It takes a lot of emotional strength to grow into a player. Avoid negative language (e.g., should, must, unfair, unjust, etc.). Use positive language (e.g., could, might, fair, just, etc.).

3. Use pain and frustration to build strength. Ask, "What challenges am I facing?" rather than "What happened to me?"

4. Do not blame. Do not judge. Take responsibility for the process in your organization. It doesn't matter who created the process.

5. For each solution, ask, "What worked well?" and "What could be improved?"

6. Learn from your experiences. The only failure is when you do not learn from your mistakes.

7. Share information before someone needs it. Openness and transparency create a trusting and proactive environment.

8. Take the initiative. Don't wait to be asked to do something.

9. Give credit where credit is due. Praising others for their contribution, no matter how small, will go a long way to building trust. Many point out that a kind word and thoughtful gesture are the two most powerful things. Use them and use them often.

10. Use common sense to build a common practice. Build upon the above points to implement effective and efficient methods in your organization.

Implementing the above will help you build space, safety, and comfort in the organization so that others become players. In essence, you're changing the beliefs and values of the organization one person at a time until all behaviors align to create a quality culture of efficiency, effectiveness, and productivity. This approach is how one changes organizational culture.

Next time you encounter a problem, stick around. It's a perfect opportunity to grow, learn, and improve your player skills.

What is Value-Add and How Does it Impact Efficiency?

What is 'value add,' and how does it impact efficiency? To answer this question, let me first explain what 'value add' means. Something value added (or adding value) must meet three criteria:

1. The customer is willing to pay for it.
2. A process, object, or service has to be physically changed.
3. The process, object, or service is made/done right *the first time.*

In short, value added is anything not wasted. What is interesting and perhaps surprising is that in many organizations, most activities included in processes are non-value-adding activities. Estimates peg only about five percent as an actual value add, with the rest wasting time and money.

In Lean, there are eight types of waste. Some organizations also talk about seven or nine wastes, but generally, eight is common. They include defects, overproduction, waiting, non-utilized talent, transportation, inventory, motion, and extra-processing – an easy way to recall these wastes is to use the acronym DOWNTIME. Let me give you a quick overview of each type of waste.

- Defects could be anything ranging from incorrect parts or services not delivered to the customers' specifications to errors in documentation. Common causes of defects include lack of process controls, poor quality of incoming materials, poor work instructions, inadequate training, or other reasons.

- Overproduction includes anything produced faster, sooner, or more than needed. Overproduction leads to high costs.

- Waiting is time lost when people, materials, or machines are waiting for service or the next step in the process.

- Non-utilized talent is wasted potential for improvement. It results when the organization does not consult its staff for ideas on improving the work methods. Some causes of this include old-guard thinking, politics, business culture, or no training.

- Transportation of parts and materials around a facility can create waste. Some causes of this waste include poor plant layouts, large batch sizes, or large storage areas.

- Inventory is any material more than the one piece required for the next step in production. The most significant reason inventory is in excess is that people hold stock "just in case" they may need it.

- Motion is the movement of people or machines above what is needed to do the job. For example, poor workplace organization and housekeeping, poor workstation layouts, and sorting or looking for items are all causes of wasted motion.

- Extra-processing is about doing more than the minimum required to transform the material into an acceptable product. For example, over-packaging is an extra-processing waste. Some causes of extra-processing include redundant approvals or inspections, unnecessary reports, or accommodating perceived customer needs.

Now, considering value add as anything that is not waste, and waste falling into one of the above eight categories, consider your organization's efficiencies. How much waste is in your processes? As mentioned, the typical organization without a Lean transformation has only about five percent value-added activities in its processes. Therefore, 95 percent of the activities are waste. Hence, there is room for at least a 95 percent improvement in efficiency in each process. That is a considerable number. Equally astounding is that these wastes equate to lost time and money on a large scale.

So, what is value add, and how does it impact efficiency? Value add means removing waste from your processes to improve efficiency and the bottom line. Discipline yourself and your organization to get Lean to eliminate waste and improve process efficiencies.

The Power of Why

One of the best ways to get to the root causes of problems lies in the question of why. Why does it take 30 days to pay an invoice? Why does Finance require five signatures on the cheque? Why is the Contracts Division involved in payment processing? Why? It is such a simple question, but it can generate powerful results.

The key to using the 5-Whys is to ask "why" five times (sometimes the answer you're looking for will appear in less than five questions, but usually not more than five). Each why question builds on the answer provided to the previous question. Here's an example of how to use it to get to the root causes of problems, starting with the problem statement.

Problem statement: Our suppliers are unhappy because they aren't getting their payments within two weeks of invoicing.

1. Why aren't suppliers getting paid within two weeks?

Finance takes at least two weeks to get approvals on the invoice.

2. Why does it take Finance at least two weeks to approve the invoice?

The contract manager needs at least two weeks to approve the invoice.

3. Why does it take at least two weeks for the contract manager to approve the invoice?

The contract manager doesn't always get notified about product/service receipts.

4. Why doesn't the contract manager get product/service receipt notifications?

I don't know.

In this case, payment delay results from inadequate product/service receipt notification. Thus, our starting point for exploring the problem is this notification lapse.

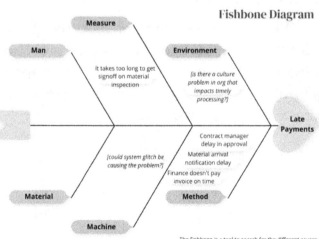

The Fishbone is a tool to search for the different causes of a problem. This visual tool resembles a fish skeleton graphically to represent the causes leading to a situation or a problem.

The 5 Whys can also be part of a cause-and-effect diagram. This diagram is also known as a fishbone or Ishikawa diagram. Here is an example.

You will notice that process (i.e., method) has the most issues, indicating that process may be the root cause of the problem you seek to resolve. Evaluating my fishbone diagram above, you may consider that some of the items under "method" could fall under "material" or "man" (or "people") issues, which is fair. For instance, is the contract manager's delay in approval the result of the process/method or a personal matter? Is the material arrival delayed notification due to the process or material issue? These are questions that those closest to the operation can decipher more clearly. My intent with the diagram was to show how to use it with the 5-Whys.

While a straightforward tool, the power of the 5-Whys in rooting out causes of problems is invaluable to those interested in improving organizational processes. It is simply one of the most accessible tools to use.

Distinguishing Between Needs and Requirements

Understanding what your customers need and what they require is imperative for productivity. Determining between the two will take your company from being an average organization to a top-notch organization. The first thing to understand regarding needs and requirements is your customer. How does one define a customer?

Simply put, a customer is a recipient of a product or service you or your organization provide. Of note is that a customer can be internal or external to an organization. For example, if you work in a large organization, your operations department is a customer of the finance department, and vice versa, depending on the service.

When focusing on your customers, first, it is critical to understand each customer's impact on your business. This understanding includes the customer's loyalty to your company (short or long-term customer), their location (local or international), and the type of product or service they require from your business.

Next, you must understand the difference between your customer's needs and requirements. A customer need establishes the relationship between you or your organization and the customer. A need is the customer's underlying desires, problems, or goals the customer seeks to address through a particular product or service. Needs are the broad, sometimes emotional, factors that drive customers to purchase or find a solution.

On the other hand, a requirement determines whether your customer is happy with the product or service. Requirements are specific, tangible, and often quantifiable characteristics of a product or service that meets the customer's needs. Requirements are customer expectations. Let me give you an example.

If you run a hotel and a guest (your customer) orders coffee, it is easy to see that the customer needs coffee. However, while the need is coffee, the requirements (that *you* need to determine) are the inclusion of cream, sugar, coffee strength or type (espresso, regular, decaffeinated, etc.), correct temperature of the beverage, etc. Therefore, a need and a requirement are two distinct categories.

There are six ways we can determine the customer's needs and requirements. They include interviews, focus groups, market research, surveys, observations, and customer complaints.

Interviews are typically more detailed questions and responses and are usually one-on-one connections than focus groups. A key advantage of interviews over focus groups is an opportunity for a deeper conversation.

A drawback of focus groups is that they may present a halo or devil effect. Thus, responses may not be as genuine as in a one-on-one interview. Note that a halo effect is the tendency of someone's impressions in one area to affect their opinions positively or negatively in other areas. For example, we see the halo effect if a focus group participant doesn't like their boss; they may also dislike the organization and provide negative responses about organizational strategies. The devil effect is a reverse halo effect where one disliked trait of a person or product negatively influences all attributes of that person or product. For example, if a participant doesn't like that their boss is rude to some employees, they may think their boss is disrespectful to everyone.

Market research is beneficial because it provides a larger sample size and quantitative data. However, this type of research can be expensive. On the other hand, surveys can provide quick and specific information with a large sample. Unfortunately, surveys tend to generate low response rates; any response rate less than 10 percent is insufficient.

Finally, customer observations and complaints likely provide the best opportunities to gather unfiltered and accurate data. They also allow the organization to observe the customer's body language—even if they don't say everything they think about your product or service, you can fill in the blanks by observing their body language (much like in interviews and focus groups). Regarding complaints, if the complaint recurs, this is a good indicator of a need or requirement.

Once you have determined your customers' needs and requirements, it is important to prioritize them into four areas: must-haves, nice-to-haves, delighters, and frustraters. The "must-haves" are something in the service or product that the customer might not notice, but they would notice its absence. For example, your coffee order arrives while you're sitting in a restaurant, but the server does not bring cream, sugar, or a teaspoon. You would likely notice the absence of the cream, sugar, or teaspoon (i.e., the "must-haves").

The nice-to-have is not something that the customer might notice right away, but the more they experience it, the more they will see it. For example, if you are a restaurant owner and Joe regularly visits your restaurant, calling Joe by his first name when he orders coffee is a nice-to-have. It helps build customer relationships; it's a "nice-have."

A delighter is something that you provide, but your competition does not. For example, perhaps your restaurant offers customized meal orders, not on your standard menu—that is a delighter. In today's world of more conscious eaters, offering customized meals would undoubtedly go a long way to delighting customers and building a loyal following.

Finally, a frustrator is something that you or your organization think is a requirement, but it irritates the customer, or the customer is indifferent to it. For example, over-packaging items because you think they look pretty might detract from the customer's satisfaction. Also, over-packaging requires more time and effort to unwrap items, resulting in more waste. I have experienced this with certain brands of face creams and chocolates.

Ultimately, customer needs are the why behind a purchase or problem resolution, while requirements are the what or how a product or service will fulfill the needs. Understanding your customers' needs and requirements leads to greater customer satisfaction and better business outcomes for your organization.

Project Charter – Why Do We Need One, Anyway?

Clients often ask me why they need a project charter. After all, if we're working on the project (or if the project was our idea), we certainly know what to do, don't we? Yes and no. While organizations, individuals, and project managers may know what they need to do, the project charter is an essential tool that provides purpose and motivation for a team to do its work. It is the "guiding hand" for completing the project.

There are six elements in a good project charter: business case, problem statement, project scope, goals and objectives, milestones, and roles and responsibilities. Project charters may have additional elements, but these six are key. Here is what these elements contribute to the project.

1. The business case describes the project's activities and how it impacts the organization's strategic business objectives. The business case is typically motivational to explain why the project is worth doing. For example, "The planning department is experiencing increasing challenges in issuing building permits in a reasonable

timeframe. This delay is directly contributing to decreased revenues for the organization."

2. The problem statement identifies the problem that the project will address. The problem statement is specific and measurable, indicates how long the problem has existed, and describes the gap between the current and desired states. For example, "In the past five years, the number of building permits issued has decreased by 50 percent due to the high turnaround time for processing. Turnaround time for issuing building permits needs to be improved by 50 percent within the next year."

3. Project scope defines the boundaries of the project work. It also helps avoid scope creep, which occurs when the team starts working on activities outside the project scope. The project scope helps the team avoid working on projects that "boil the ocean" (i.e., doing everything all at once). For example, "The project includes a review of building permits issued by the planning department over the past five years, and developing and implementing processes to improve turnaround time for building permits issued by the planning department. Not included in the scope – all other types of permits issued by the organization."

4. Goals and objectives in the project charter identify what the team/project will accomplish and within what timeframe. For example, "1. Reduce turnaround time for permit issuing, 2. Improve planning department building permit issuing processes, and 3. Review and recommend changes to forms used in building permit processes."

5. Milestones are dates the project manager and sponsor assign to each goal. They help the team stay on track and are essential for overall project completion.

6. Roles and responsibilities are a crucial part of the project charter. In all instances, the project needs a project champion. This person allocates resources, removes obstacles, and identifies the project team. In addition, the project requires a project manager (internal or external) and an internal team leader. Of course, the project team is essential, but keep the number of team members to eight or fewer to better manage the overall project.

Use the project charter to help you manage your project and meet deliverables. It is a living document for a live project, which could save your life on the project. It is your key to keeping the project within a specified boundary relating to deliverables, resources, and timeframes.

Preventing Projects from Going Sideways

Your project is humming along when, without warning, the scope expands. This expansion may or may not be good in the consulting world. However, scope creep can be a real problem within organizations—usually hurting the bottom line.

The secret to controlling scope creep is to control it from day one of the project. This control means ensuring that you thoroughly understand the project's deliverables and carefully track that all efforts go into only those deliverables. When you notice work occurring outside of scope, immediately stop the project. Examine why things are off track and re-focus.

Follow these five guidelines to help you successfully control your project's scope.

1. Understand the project. Before writing the project charter, make sure you understand (really understand) the project's deliverables. Ask for and ensure you get all the information you need to understand the project.

2. Build a Gantt chart[2] complete with time and resources. Understanding the tasks involved

in the project is critical to writing the project charter. This understanding includes anticipated timelines and resources for each task. A Gantt chart can be a powerful tool for immediately visualizing the project's requirements.

3. Write the project charter. With the completed Gantt chart, you can now write the project charter. The charter should include relevant information you and your team can use to manage the project. This information includes project scope definition (covering project inclusions and exclusions – be specific), assumptions, objectives, deliverables, organizational scope, timeframe, team and other stakeholders, risk management strategies, communication plan, and a change management plan.

4. Work on the project based on the approved project charter.

5. Manage project changes using the strategies outlined in the project charter.

A final word: Expect that there will be scope creep. Sometimes, projects evolve into more extensive undertakings as they progress. This evolution is not a problem if you manage the change effectively. Refer to your project charter for appropriate change management measures, including obtaining necessary approvals and adjusting your timelines and resources before continuing the project.

By informing everyone about project progress regularly (usually weekly or monthly), you can quickly catch potential changes or problems and adjust the project accordingly.

Here's to your project's success!

Changing Behavior by Changing Situations

You've probably heard it before: "He's so stubborn." "She won't listen." "They just don't seem to get how this new product will help them with their work." "They're so negative." When dealing with those who resist change, this innuendo is familiar. But it may surprise you that people are not always the problem in resistance to change. More frequently, the situation, not the person, is the common cause.

For example, in their study[3] on mindless eating, Brian Wansink and his colleagues at Cornell provided moviegoers with free, bottomless large or medium-sized popcorn buckets. Generally, the researchers believed the individuals could not eat all the popcorn with the intentionally large portion sizes. In addition, the popcorn was stale and popped five days ago. The researchers wanted to investigate how visual cues and portion sizes influenced people's eating behaviors.

The researchers found surprising results. Despite moviegoers with bottomless popcorn buckets eating much more popcorn due to the continuous refilling, they appeared unaware of their increased consumption. The researchers hypothesized people with larger buckets would eat more popcorn. Their hypothesis was correct. The bigger the bucket, the bigger the eater: they ate 53 percent more!

Viewing the data without knowing the difference in bucket sizes, you might easily conclude that 53 percent of moviegoers eat a lot of popcorn. Or that popcorn intake is 53 percent higher at movie theatres than at other venues, and so on. You may even start thinking about ways to motivate these gluttons to change to healthier ways of eating.

Notice that as we jump to conclusions, we immediately think about how to change the person or the person's behavior. We don't usually delve into the situation to understand what caused the behavior in the first place. In this experiment, the bucket size contributed to the popcorn eaten. Therefore, change the situation, and you change the behavior: Change the bucket size, and people will eat less popcorn. How easy is that?

When one changes the situation, there is no need to act on the individual to motivate or cajole them into changing their behavior. The new condition allows the individual to change their behavior without perhaps knowing that they've changed.

For example, many people struggle with email, claiming it interferes with their work. Each time an email pops up, they feel compelled to check it because it might be urgent (note: if it's coming via email, I can assure you it is not critical). One easy fix for this scenario is to turn off your email notification screen so you won't get an alert each time a new email arrives. Another option is to turn off your email while concentrating on other work and only check your email twice a day: first thing in the morning and just before closing for the day.

Want to eat less? Use a smaller plate. Want to be more friendly to customers in your office? Rearrange your furniture so your computer doesn't block your view of the customer. Want to spend less money? Give yourself an allowance each week/month, and stop when you've spent the budget.

Next time you face resistance to change, look at the environment (like your email or the organization of the furniture in your office). What situation can you change to achieve the desired outcome? The solution may be as easy as changing bucket sizes.

Resistance is Futile

For *Star Trek* fans, the title of this blog will feel familiar. The show's alien species, the Borg, made the saying "resistance is futile" famous in popular culture (well, for Baby Boomers, anyway!). The saying is a core concept in the Borg's quest for perfection through the forced assimilation of individuals. These forced assimilations have no place in the real world, but sometimes organizational change initiatives might feel like the Borg is in control. It does not have to be this way.

When organizations undertake change initiatives, they answer three questions:

1. What to change?

2. To what to change?

3. How do we make the change happen?

The first two questions are typically easy to answer. It's question three that usually stumps individuals and organizations. Question three is where resistance is usually most prevalent.

Resistance to change occurs when the organization does not address one or more layers of resistance during the change process. These layers of resistance arise in any of the above questions (or phases) and involve inadequate resolution of one or more of the following situations:

- Lack of agreement on the problem.

- Lack of agreement on a possible direction for a solution.

- Lack of agreement that the solution will truly address the problem.

- Concern that the solution will lead to new undesirable side effects ("Yes, but...").

- Lack of a clear path around obstacles blocking the solution.

- Lack of follow-through even after agreement to proceed with the solution (unverbalized fear or concerns).

Astute leaders address the layers of resistance to gain (or re-gain) support for change when there is resistance to change. They demonstrate a whole-system view of the problem's root cause and solutions. Some solutions to resistance to change lay in the theory of constraints thinking[4] processes. Using integrated problem-solving tools based on rigorous cause-and-effect logic can create breakthrough solutions by identifying, challenging, and correcting unexamined assumptions.

In a nutshell, consider sufficiency and necessity logic, including tree diagrams to address each resistance layer. For example, "If . . . then . . . because . . . " explains why situations exist or why we believe specific actions will result in inevitable outcomes. Further, using "To . . . , we must . . . ," we can associate requirements with desired outcomes. Thus, organizations can streamline operations, reduce waste, and improve their overall performance by identifying and addressing constraints.

The thinking tools are an excellent way to encourage collaboration and dialogue, resulting in common-sense outcomes for all participants. They also help link the three questions of change into a seamless process that provides meaningful and robust improvements in the organization.

Using the theory of constraints thinking to implement change can eliminate resistance, and individuals will not feel like resistance is futile. Nor will assimilation feel like such a bad thing.

Brainstorming—Not for Everyone

Many of us have participated in brainstorming exercises at some point in our business careers. Brainstorming seems to be the preferred technique by which organizations generate creative ideas and solutions for problems. However, it may surprise you that brainstorming is no more effective for developing ideas than having individuals work independently.

Alex Osborn, author of the 1948 book *Your Creative Power*,[5] popularized brainstorming. However, a study[6] in 1958 at Yale University refuted Osborn's claim that many of us work more creatively in teams. The study found that those who worked independently devised twice as many solutions as brainstorming groups, and their solutions were more effective.

Keith Sawyer, a psychologist at Washington University in St. Louis, suggests that decades of research show that groups engaged in brainstorming generate significantly fewer ideas than individuals who work alone and then combine their ideas.[7] In other words, brainstorming does not unleash the group's potential but makes everyone less creative.

While rules are essential when working with groups, perhaps the most inhibiting constraint to creativity is not criticizing others' ideas. The rules for brainstorming (as originated by Osborn) are:

1. Come up with as many ideas as you can.

2. Do not criticize one another's ideas.

3. Free-wheel and share wild ideas.

4. Expand and elaborate on existing ideas.

If group members are not allowed to criticize ideas, how is creativity expected to flourish? Certainly, reviewing ideas later is an option (typically after a brainstorming session), but it is far more creative to dispel wrong notions from the onset.

Charlan Nemeth,[8] a psychologist at the University of California at Berkeley, has repeatedly shown that groups engaging in debate and dissent come up with approximately 25 percent more ideas than those engaging in brainstorming. In addition, individuals and organizations typically rate these ideas as more original and valuable.

Using criticism depends on the makeup of the brainstorming group. Members who are comfortable and well-known to each other may benefit from a bout of criticism of ideas while engaging in lively idea generation. However, allowing criticism when there are new members or where members are highly introverted may do more harm than good.

From my perspective, there are two ways in which brainstorming can be effective:

1. Creative brainstorming occurs with members who are comfortable with accepting and giving criticism.

2. An effective facilitator must guide the group to allow an invigorating debate of ideas and enable participants to be honest about what ideas are good and which do not merit further consideration.

There is no need to suffer through rubbish ideas during brainstorming. And if you happen to be on the receiving end of the thumbs down for your idea, do not become offended. Remember that the thumbs-down is not for you but for your idea. We all occasionally have good and bad ideas.

Business Value in a Post-Pandemic World

Let's face it. The COVID-19 pandemic made us retreat inward, seeking solace from those closest to us, pivoting to embrace value—the value of family, friends, colleagues, neighbors, and others—those significant others who enabled our happiness and stability in an unstable world.

At the same time, businesses retreated inward, looking to salvage or expand their value. For the typical business owner, the pandemic meant staff downsizing, reducing operational hours, and cutting purchase costs while attempting to keep sales at or better than pre-pandemic levels. Now that the world is in the post-pandemic stage, individuals and businesses are returning to normal. But for companies, normal may not mean what it did pre-pandemic.

Many experts will tell you that the keys to business success include improving leadership, going digital, building a network, upskilling your staff, building a strategy, and so on. While all these tips are excellent and necessary for any business, one key element is missing: *value*. Specifically, what value does your business provide your customers? Unfortunately, most companies are so focused on looking inward and improving their processes that they forget about their customers. But without customers, you have no business.

You might say, sure, customers are essential, but your business needs to be cost-effective; otherwise, you won't be profitable. Fair point. But have you thought about your business value from the customer's perspective?

The Merriam-Webster dictionary provides eight definitions for value. The definitions relate to market price, luminosity, and denomination. From a business perspective, value relates to market price and the customer's perception of a fair return on an exchange. However, from the perspective of a *thriving* business, the customer signals value through the products and services they purchase from your business.

If you're a Lean organization, you know all about customer value, but non-Lean organizations sometimes struggle to determine their customers' value. However, determining value is not difficult. It comes down to ensuring that the business meets the customers' expectations – all the time. Look at it this way:

- An organization with efficient processes can keep its costs down. Lower costs mean a remarkable ability to attract more customers, translating to paying less.

- An organization with inefficient processes incurs higher production costs. These costs get transferred to the customer. The customer does not see this as value.

- Customers who value your products or services will pay your asking price. If your offering does not meet your customers' criteria for value, the customer may still pay for it, but they will be shopping around next time they want the same thing.

Next time you complete a transaction with your customer, ask them to rate the value they just received from you. Their response will tell you how well you are doing compared to how well you think you're doing. Consider it a reality check.

Inefficiency can be a business killer, but so can an inability to recognize value from the customers' perspective. To get an edge on the competition post-pandemic, be the customer of your business to determine your business value. When you do, you will unleash your business' unlimited potential.

MEASURE

Peak Performers: Not Always Good for Business

Are you a peak performer? According to organizational psychology, the five fundamental peak performance proficiencies are:

- Awareness of self in all domains

- Control of effort

- Visualization

- Cognitive skills

- Self-programming

These proficiencies are standard in all top achievers. However, being a top achiever on a team may be counterproductive when all other members are not top achievers. Why? One team member working harder (or less hard) than other members hinders workflow. In their book *Learning to See*, Mike Rother and John Shook[9] illustrate this concept.

Imagine a team of rowers in a boat. Each member must pull the oar through the water as smoothly as possible with the force and frequency dictated by the cox. However, each rower must have a different strength depending on their position in the boat. The person in the bow seat must also be precise because the boat goes wherever the bow goes. Thus, any deviation in this rower's stroke could send the boat off course. The same thing occurs with people and processes in organizations.

If synchronized, a system's parts (or team members) enable the system to run smoothly. This synchronization means that no one piece of the system is running faster or slower than it should. What this means for service or manufacturing settings is a requirement for workflow balance among all individuals if the organization is to function efficiently.

There is a prevalence of advice on managing underperforming employees, but an equivalent amount of literature is lacking for managing over-performers. Perhaps this is because organizations do not generally see over-performance as a problem. While this balance can be a problem in teams, especially in manufacturing, it can also affect service.

I am not espousing that everyone should be an underperformer—far from it! Organizations can benefit if they ensure their systems are waste-free (especially travel and motion waste) so their employees can be as efficient as possible. By eliminating waste and creating flow, underperformers and over-performers can work together more productively, creating an efficient workflow.

Performance psychology teaches us that workers want to succeed in an organization. By extension, these same workers want the organization to succeed. What is not clear is what motivates workers to want this success. Regardless, organizations must remember that their front-line workers are often the face (or voice) of the organization's brand to the customer. Organizations that provide their workers with tools and systems that enable efficiency will help their workers continue to succeed. It's that simple.

Leaning for Success

Lean is a management philosophy aimed at reducing waste—a philosophy that, to be effective, must become second nature to the way we work. We can trace Lean's roots to the early 1900s. However, American businessman John Krafcik coined the term Lean in 1988,[10] later defined by American researchers James Womack and Daniel Jones in 1996.[11]

Lean has several elements, but four fundamental principles will help kick-start a Lean initiative. They are:

1. Takt time

2. Standard work

3. One-piece flow

4. Pull systems.

Here's how each principle contributes to your organization's Lean initiative.

Takt time (takt: German for "beat" or "measure," which refers to music) tells organizations how many products or services the organization must produce/deliver based on customer demand. The formula to calculate takt time is:

Takt time = available time/customer demand

One can use this equation for any frequency of time and ·customer demand; however, typically, organizations use daily amounts.

When you know how much time is available to meet customer demand, you know exactly how much time you need to develop each product or service. Knowing takt time allows you to see the waste and related strategic opportunities. For example, assume that one department employs three staff to process orders. You calculate that the department has 900 minutes of available time each day, i.e., (3 employees × 480 minutes per day)–(3 employees × 60 minutes for lunch). You also estimate that it takes 30 minutes to process each order, and there are 25 orders each day.

Therefore, 30 minutes multiplied by 25 orders equals 750 minutes—but your staff is available for 900 minutes. The strategic opportunity is determining what to do with the remaining 150 minutes. Do you reduce staff working hours, reallocate staff to another area, choose how to increase customer demand, etc.?

The following principle, standard work, ensures that all work follows written standards and procedures. Standard work is necessary to ensure that anyone doing the job does it the same way, i.e., standard work. Having procedures in place to ensure standard work is the basis for improvement in any organization.

The third principle, one-piece flow, is difficult for organizations because most organizations think along traditional functional hierarchies. A one-piece flow system co-locates all services relating to the value stream in one department based on the logical sequence of work. For example, consider parking tickets. In the traditional organization, one department issues parking tickets (e.g., Bylaw Enforcement), another collects payment (e.g., Finance), and yet another department handles parking ticket challenges or complaints (e.g., Legal).

However, in a one-piece flow system, people work side-by-side to handle all parking ticket issues, e.g., the Parking Department. Therefore, completing the parking ticket process takes days instead of months in a one-piece flow.

The final critical fundamental principle, pull systems, is simple but challenging to implement. In a pull system, the organization provides products and services to customers when needed. Therefore, the organization only starts filling customer orders when the customer places the order and not before, drawing on inventory as required.

Workers develop products and services based on anticipated customer demands in a traditional organization with a push system. In this instance, inventory becomes a real problem regarding space utilization for inventory storage and the associated costs of carrying (and, perhaps, destroying) stock.

As you implement Lean in your organization, remember these fundamental principles and return to them when things go off-track. No matter the nature of your organization—private or public—treat all the work you do as a business, and you'll find the Lean principles much easier to apply.

In God we Trust; for Everything Else, There's Data

Statistics are all about data. But did you know that one could manipulate data to provide hypothesized results? Don't get me wrong. I believe data is fundamental. Without it, we'd be hard-pressed to provide evidence in specific situations. However, if one does not collect data in a controlled manner, the data can be useless. Let me explain.

Collecting data requires an understanding of the data's purpose. In business settings, the place to start is to identify low-performing processes. Collecting data on these processes will provide evidence for process improvement areas. Here are some basic steps to help you with your data collection plan.

1. Measure. Identify what you will measure. Is it order entry speed, service quality, number of customer complaints, time to process help desk alerts, etc.? Be specific.

2. Type of measure. The kind of measure relates to what you are measuring and can also tell you when you have enough data. For instance, if you're measuring the quality of service, you will possibly measure one or

two inputs to the service plus two or three outputs of the service and one process measure. The key is to focus on the vital few versus the useful many. Usually, only two or three items will account for over 80% of what is essential to the customer, and that's what you need to measure.

3. Type of data. The type of data relates to discrete or continuous data. Generally, continuous data is preferred because it gives you information about magnitude. Examples of continuous data are time and temperature.

4. Operational definition. An operational definition is vital to determine when data collection starts and stops. If measuring time to complete order entry, when do you start your timer, and when do you stop? Is it when the order entry clerk receives the order or when the customer places it? In this case, you can see how being precise will enable you to collect the correct data.

There are other considerations in a data collection plan, but the above four are vital in ensuring that the data you collect serves the intended purposes. Other considerations when collecting data for process improvement include identifying specifications (i.e., the least acceptable measure in the process, such as 30 minutes is the upper limit for order entry) and targets (i.e., what customers would consider ideal – this is not always achievable, but it's good to have stretch goals).

When collecting data, ensure that you have good measurements, which means that data should be easy to understand, necessary to the customer (directly or indirectly), and the data motivate people to action.

Mapping the Inefficient Subprocess

When I prepare a high-level process map for an organizational process, I usually need at least one more map for a subprocess. The subprocess selected for review is always one that immediately surfaces as inefficient. But whether I am mapping a high-level or subprocess, the steps for mapping are the same. These seven steps are:

1. Name the process. For example, if you're mapping the high-level financial management process, you would name the process "Financial Management." If you're mapping a subprocess of Financial Management, such as invoice payment, then you would call this process "Invoice Payment."

2. Identify the start and stop points. Every process must have a start and stop point; it is imperative to identify them because they will impact your project scope. For example, the financial management process will start with, perhaps, the development of the chart of accounts and stop with year-end reporting. The invoice payment process would begin with receiving an invoice for payment and stop with payment issued. Knowing your process start and stop points,

you simultaneously identify your project scope.

3. Identify the process output. When naming the output of the process, it should be with an unqualified noun. For instance, say "payment issued, not "big payment issued." Distinguishing between the two will impact your project scope. Using a qualifier limits your scope and may exclude actual areas of inefficiencies.

4. Identify the customers of the process. Every process must have at least one customer; otherwise, you need to ask why the organization is doing the process in the first place. When identifying customers, be sure to determine all levels of customers. For example, for the invoice payment process, the customers would include the vendor (as the primary customer). However, the organization would also have internal customers such as the manager who approves the invoice for payment and other accounting staff who might code, review, and approve the invoice before issuing payment.

5. Identify the suppliers of the process. For example, suppliers in the Invoice Payment process would include banks with whom the company coordinates payment transfers, printing companies that supply

printed cheques, and others. It is crucial to identify all suppliers because once you map the process, for example, you might notice inefficiencies directly attributable to suppliers.

6. Identify the process inputs. Inputs include information provided by suppliers. For example, the bank is the supplier and provides the means to transfer funds. Perhaps the IT Department is also a supplier since it allows for the systems that enable efficient communications. Inputs can occur at any stage and more than once in the process – at the beginning, middle, or end. It all depends on the nature of the input.

7. Identify five to seven highest level steps in the process *as it exists today*. A common mistake teams make during process mapping is to draw a process the way it should be instead of the way it is. They do this because they want to improve the process while mapping. However, restraint is essential here. You need to map the entire process *as it is* before you can step back to identify areas for improvement.

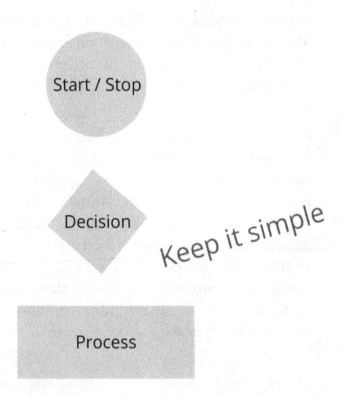

A final point about process mapping is to use standard symbols. An oval indicates start/stop points, a diamond shape is for decision points (such as yes/no, go/no go), rectangle shapes describe the step in the process, and arrows indicate the direction.

Whether mapping a high-level or subprocess, the process map is a powerful tool to help quickly visualize improvement areas. The benefits of process mapping include identifying opportunities, significantly reducing expenses, simplifying workflow, improving cross-functional communication, identifying root causes of problems, and more.

Even if you think your organization's processes are running smoothly, map out a process every few months and see how much you can save in time and money; I'll bet you dollars to donuts, you'll discover non-value-added tasks and costs. By removing them, you'll be boosting your organization's efficiency, productivity, and bottom line.

Tradition and Productivity

In the acclaimed Broadway musical *Fiddler on the Roof*, the main character, Tevye, explains his society's traditions in the song "Tradition." The piece juxtaposes village life with a world that is changing around them. In many respects, struggles faced in today's organizations may be rooted in difficulty in letting go of tradition—an inability to change.

Consider that the world's most successful organizations have one thing in common: they can adapt quickly to change. The fact that half of the top 20 companies in the world are all in the field of technology[12] is telling: companies that have embraced technology are the companies that continue to lead in earnings and productivity.

To improve performance and productivity, companies use technology and its related gadgets. However, its usefulness is limited if the technology does not provide helpful information to the user and the organization. Technological tools must be able to provide information about performance in both directions. Let me give you an example.

Some companies implemented a web-based timesheet manager that included two measures of productivity on projects—one for the employee and the other for their team. While the system encouraged productivity, it only measured performance one way—how the organization determined to be correct. In this example, timesheets only measured what the organization wanted; they ignored employee input. Meeting targets is one thing, but did the employee or team agree to the targets in the first place? Are the targets realistic? How has meeting the targets impacted employee well-being or team morale? These and other considerations are imperative in performance measures to improve the activities that comprise productivity.

The approach described is typical of many organizations. By all accounts, it is traditional and one-way—company to employee.

The company's demands for maximum productivity must couple with meeting employee needs. This approach includes understanding the individual and their work and what they need to get the job done. In other words, companies need to listen to their employees before developing systems. This approach is especially true in today's economy, where Generations X and Y have displaced the Baby Boomers in the workforce.

Successful organizations must change their systems and processes to meet the needs of the "what's in it for me" generation (X) and the Gen Y kids, who are very technology-wise and immune to most traditional marketing and sales pitches.

The tradition carried into the workplace by Baby Boomers no longer meets the needs of organizations.

Insisting on maintaining practices started in the twentieth century is not a tradition that will benefit twenty-first-century companies. The successful organizations of the twenty-first century will want to work with their employees to learn how to accomplish more for the benefit of the employees and the organization.

Leveraging the Power of Stakeholders

Do you know that excitement that goes along with your great idea for improving your organization's processes? From great idea to project charter, your momentum is at a peak when you present your project charter to the project champion for approval. At this point, your project can go one of two ways: approval or rejection. If it's approved, great! You're on your way to making changes. If rejected, there is a strong likelihood that you did not engage and secure the support of all stakeholders.

We often talk about engaging and getting buy-in from stakeholders. But what, exactly, does this mean? Let's start by defining a stakeholder. Stakeholders are all people interested in your project and affected by your work. They can include, for example, senior managers, colleagues, customers, suppliers, banks, government(s), unions, community groups, and others.

Consider these critical steps for determining and evaluating your stakeholders:

1. Brainstorm to identify your stakeholders. As you brainstorm with your team, you may develop unique stakeholder categories.

2. Prioritize stakeholders based on their power and interest in your project.

3. Understand what motivates your stakeholders and what actions you need to take to persuade them to support your project.

After identifying your stakeholders, determine their power. That is, what is their desire and ability to influence your project? Stakeholders can disrupt your plans, cause uncertainty, or be your staunchest advocate. In short, businesses need and rely on their stakeholders.

Understanding and leveraging stakeholder power and interest is vital in getting project support (or buy-in). The matrix at the end of this article provides an overview of power and interest. It illustrates the following:

- If a stakeholder has high power and high interest, they are a vital player. Take notice and collaborate with them to achieve project success. You must fully engage them and make a significant effort to satisfy their needs regarding the project.

- If a stakeholder has high power and low interest, involve them in the project by regularly communicating with them or asking them how they wish to be involved/informed.

- If a stakeholder has low power and high interest, communicate frequently with them. These people can be helpful with project details.

- If a stakeholder has low power and low interest, monitor their input as necessary to the project's success.

With the above in mind, identify your stakeholders and how they fit in the power–interest matrix. The best way to determine this is to meet with them and ask them directly—this is a significant first step to building a successful relationship.

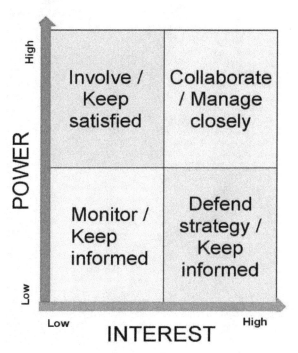

Knowing all the above—your stakeholders, their power and interest in your project, and their motivation—you can now use an appropriate method of engagement to win their support for your project and its success.

In addition, don't forget to review your power–interest grid to ensure that stakeholder influence has not changed. If it has, contact your stakeholders and determine how you can maintain their project support.

Almighty Surveys

If you're like most executives (i.e., more than 80 percent),[13] you rely on surveys to collect data about and from your customers. There is also a good chance that you use at least three to five data sources (including surveys) to get this information. Surveys[14] outrank other data collection methods because of their coverage and independence of observations. If worded correctly, surveys can answer specific questions precisely, and organizations can analyze and track data over time. Who doesn't want to know how their customers behave and how their behavior affects (or will affect) the organization?

While the almighty survey is still Number One, it can be costly and time-consuming, and the responses do not provide the details needed for action planning and implementation. For this, the organization would need to undergo further information gathering (e.g., focus groups and/or in-depth interviews) and, typically, outsourcing to consultants to build appropriate go-forward plans.

If you are using surveys, here are some things to consider to maximize the value of the responses:[15]

1. Provide an incentive. One company included a letter with the survey stating that any person who completed the survey would have a $25 contribution sent to the Children's Make a Wish fund in their name. Their response rate was close to 90 percent and generated tremendous goodwill.

2. Think: What's in it for them? Don't waste participants' time with unnecessary questions. Instead, think: "What do they care about?" More companies are moving to a market research-driven survey that explores customers' future expectations and needs rather than past performance. Participants will be more apt to participate if they feel they have some impact on the direction of an organization's products or services.

3. Tailor the questions to the specific department or manager receiving the survey. If you want to improve response rates, develop particular surveys. Don't ask the purchasing department about the quality of your products or the quality department about your delivery performance unless there is a targeted reason to do so.

4. Include a short, personalized introduction letter hand-signed by someone in the organization. While we all love email, a

handwritten note is still an acceptable way to thank someone. This brief introductory letter, signed by a senior company representative, will improve the response rate.

5. Remember: Less is more. Asking someone to spend 20–30 minutes on the phone or complete a 10-page survey doesn't work. It's better to get many responses to a handful of questions than a few responses to a large number of questions. One company sent a survey with only one question: "What could we do better?" They received a 50 percent response rate.

Organizations shouldn't use surveys for everything. Other data collection methods may be better depending on your questions. For instance, if your organization wonders how well its implemented standards and specifications address key customer expectations, observations may be better than surveys. In this instance, a quality function deployment (a Lean Six Sigma tool) would deliver the best results.

Whatever method you choose, remember that surveys, if done right, can give you the correct information needed to drive improvement and your bottom line.

Eliminate DOWNTIME to Re-ignite Your Business Post Pandemic

What's your story? How did the pandemic impact your business? If you're like most businesses that did not embrace Lean before the pandemic, the pandemic likely hit your business with closures and resulting staffing and customer issues. But now that you're back at it, how do you prevent your business from experiencing havoc when the next crisis hits? I have good news for you on that front: DOWNTIME.

DOWNTIME is a fundamental approach to keeping your business lean and productive no matter what gets thrown your way. DOWNTIME stands for defects, overproduction, waiting, non-utilized talent, transportation, inventory, motion, and extra-processing. Let me break each category down for you.

In simplest terms, defects are errors. Any time you must re-do, re-write, re-format, re-manufacture, replace, etc., you are correcting something that you (or whoever was responsible) should have done correctly the first time. In other words, a defect indicates a failure in a product or service to meet agreed-to customer requirements. Defects result in wasted resources (work effort, physical materials, and time). When defects occur, they impact the quality of the product or service and, by extension, the reputation and profitability of the providing organization or individual. Thus, as a business owner, your key to quality products and services is to eliminate defects in your work system and avoid defective work from getting to the customer.

Overproduction means producing more than your customer or your internal process needs. It results in excess inventory. For instance, I have been in client offices where administrative staff created complete sets of paper file folders (sometimes in the hundreds!) in anticipation of having paper documents for those folders in the next fiscal year – clearly, a waste of time and resources for all concerned. The best way to avoid overproduction is to produce products and services when the customer (internal or external to the organization) needs them, i.e., just in time.

Waiting is a waste with which most of us are familiar. In an efficient and productive business, there should be minimal waiting on people, equipment, materials, and information – all required to complete work. I had quite an experience at a medical appointment years ago where I waited for two hours to see the doctor before walking out – I'm amazed that I waited as long as I did. To ensure your business does not hold up its customers or staff, ensure that your team is well-trained and that equipment, materials, and information are well-maintained and flowing to the right people at the right time.

Non-utilized talent is not using your staff's skills, knowledge, and experiences to improve the organization. How often have you overloaded your plate with work by not delegating to competent staff? How often have you felt you were the only one who knew how to do the job? Include your employees in your workload and train them to take on more. It will improve their skills and inspire them to do more to improve the organization's overall functioning. Involving staff in your work processes is a win–win for all concerned.

Transportation refers to the unnecessary movement of the organization's material, people, and equipment, often resulting in wasted time and possible damage. For example, look at your warehouses or other inventory stores – how are your products organized? Are you in the business of transporting goods? How do you ensure you get the right product to the right customer quickly and safely? Also, ensure your equipment is working to avoid accidents and wasted time.

Inventory cuts across many areas of the organization; when it is in excess, it takes up valuable space and requires resources to manage. In addition, it ties up your capital. Inventory is directly related to overproduction, defects, transportation, and extra-processing. Use the "just in time" ordering method to ensure you only have what you need for the immediate task. By only having what you need, you save time and money and improve your work environment (i.e., clutter-free, which leads to less stress and chaos and more money for your bottom line).

Motion is an unnecessary movement that can cause harm to people. It can also damage your equipment or create a defective product. Anything that travels an excessive distance from a starting point to where it begins work is unnecessary. For example, walking several steps daily to retrieve printed documents is excess motion, as is searching for tools and equipment and moving heavy objects from high shelves. Organizations should configure workspaces to enable efficient work and reduce unnecessary movement. For example, when work tools are well-organized, there is less chance of injury and damage to equipment and people.

Extra-processing is an interesting waste. It refers to doing more than what the customer wants or needs. It provides more for the same price. Some organizations might think this is good customer service, but it likely is not. I can think of products I sometimes purchase wrapped in an extraordinarily sturdy box with extra cardboard securing the product inside the box, cellophane paper around the box, and a ribbon around the cellophane. Do I want or need that additional wrapping? Would I be willing to pay for that extra wrapping? No, I would not. All I want is the product. Thus, extra-processing is a waste of time and materials.

With DOWNTIME knowledge, you can enable your business to become more efficient and productive while improving profitability. While DOWNTIME is a Lean concept, you don't have to be trained in Lean to understand the concepts and begin applying them to your business. But, of course, training in Lean will help in the longer term.

Measure, analyze, and eliminate your business's DOWNTIME, and be ready for whatever the world throws. Here's to your business's enduring success!

ANALYZE

Characteristics of the Perfect Team

All organizations have and can achieve great teams. A team is a group of motivated people with complementary skills and knowledge. These individuals commit to and work toward a common purpose and performance goals. In addition, team members hold themselves mutually accountable for project success.

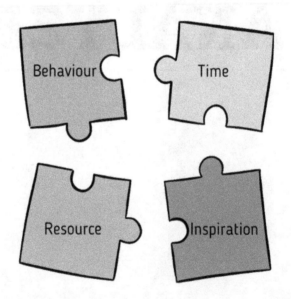

The advantages of teams outweigh the disadvantages and include harnessing collective thinking for powerful thinking. Each thought capably builds on other ideas that might develop in isolation. For instance, ten people thinking separately without the benefit of team participation equals ten or fewer individual thoughts. However, when we harness the power of those ten people sharing and building upon each other's ideas, the synergy is much greater than ten.

However, organizations and project managers should not just randomly slap together a team. Teams need training to solve problems and require continuous management support. Teams need time to develop – a room full of strangers won't gel at their first meeting. People need to know a little about each other and have time to develop. Additionally, the first teams generally need the most time to mature, and organizations should allow them to evolve at the team members' pace.

When selecting teams for projects, there are three approaches: asking for volunteers, appointing team members, or combining both techniques. Each method has pros and cons, with the best approach likely a mix of the two since that approach is more likely to acquire committed members with complementary skill sets. The only drawback is that the organization may not get enough volunteers. Regardless of the method, teams larger than eight are usually unmanageable.

Another team-building consideration is inspiration. Teams need to be goal-driven and encouraged to succeed. They must agree on shared objectives in a climate of trust and openness. They also derive inspiration from their sense of belonging to the team and value its diversity. In addition, a good team is creative and encourages risk-taking while meeting its project goals. Strong leaders who understand team dynamics can help build a perfect team.

To ensure a perfect team, the team's code of conduct should include the following elements:

- Keeping an open mind to change,

- Having a positive attitude,

- Creating a blameless environment,

- Encouraging nonjudgmental thinking,

- Fostering an awareness of multiple alternatives,

- Treating others with respect,

- Involving all team members in discussions and decisions,

- No position/ranks in teams (i.e., one person, one vote, no bosses),

- Creating a team environment,

- Considering all questions (i.e., there are no "dumb" questions),

- Creating a bias for action (i.e., just do it),

- Never leaving a meeting in silent disagreement – settle all differences at the meeting, and,

- Having fun.

Teams create and stimulate dialogue and ideas, so fun is paramount for improving creativity and progress.

Customer Service

Organizations exist to serve customers. That's obvious. What may not be as obvious is that organizations in turmoil often forget this fact.

When an organization's focus shifts from serving its customers to serving its organizational needs, problems arise. For instance, if your staff is exerting great effort to try and get customers to follow the organization's internal processes, this is a problem. Typically starting in one area of the organization, this problem can permeate like a mushroom cloud. The results can be disastrous.

Let's face it. Customers don't care about your organization's internal processes; they don't care about your processes at all. Customers want only your product(s) or service(s). How you deliver those products or services to your customer is outside of the customer's concerns. However, your customers care if they get the run around from you. Sometimes, they care enough to leave your organization altogether. These customers could be internal (e.g., staff) and external (e.g., public).

Here are some telltale signs that your organization is losing touch with its customers:

- Your staff meets customer queries with reasons or excuses about why something has or has not occurred.

- Your staff points to the customer as the problem when customers circumvent the organization's rules.

- There is a high staff turnover in your organization.

- Staff on extended sick leave is a regular occurrence.

- Work overwhelm is the norm.

- Overtime is the norm.

- Customer complaints are increasing.

- You are losing customers.

Whether from internal or external customers, treat customer complaints as an opportunity to improve services/products and your customer relationships. Here are things to consider:

1. Above all, acknowledge the customer's complaint with an apology. Don't give reasons (or excuses) for why things may have turned out the way they did. Your customer does not care about your reasons.

2. Provide options for rectifying the situation. Ask the customer if any of the options are

satisfactory. If not, ask the customer to provide alternatives.

3. Immediately follow through on delivering the agreed-upon option.

4. Check with the customer to ensure that the final delivery is satisfactory.

5. Ask for customer feedback.

6. Take customer feedback seriously. Implement organizational changes to ensure that your focus is on the customer.

It may be time for an overhaul if your internal processes regularly hinder you and your customers. Instead of experiencing up to 98% waste in your practices, why not turn that wasted time, effort, and resources into superb customer service? At the same time, you'll be saving your organization money by reducing wasted time, effort, and resources.

Be the customer! Look at your internal processes and ask yourself how you would change the process if you were the customer. You may be surprised at how much waste you might uncover in your operations in just a few minutes or hours. It won't take much money (if any) to make small process changes for significant customer satisfaction gains.

Turning Efficiency into Power

Time and again, I have spoken about the need for efficient processes and systems to enable employees to do their best. It's not enough to do something right once and then forget it. If the process or system cannot sustain efficient activity in the first place, then waste is (and will be) prevalent.

Based on a survey of 10,000 individuals in more than 400 companies,[16] individuals rated their company's ability to compete on clarity (helping individuals work smarter, not harder), navigation (assisting individuals to find who or what they need), fulfillment of basics (such as communication and knowledge management), usability (company's effectiveness in all that it designs to help people get tasks done), speed (assisting employees in working in a 24/7 ever-faster world), and their respect for employees' time. Overall, respondents reported four or more of these elements were unfavorable (67%, while only 19% reported four or more as favorable.

To put this into perspective, if you are an executive in a company of 100 employees, then:

- 52 employees must return to you to determine what you expect them to do,

- 72 can't find what they need for them to do their best,

- 75 are filling in the blanks for themselves on task/goal communication,

- 81 think their child's computer game console works better than the tools the organization supplies,

- 86 think you are like an email when pushing speed down the chain of command, but snail mail when acting on employee feedback,

- 88 have been trained by the company to guard their time, or at least to be dubious and have second thoughts or hang back when asked to give more of their time.

Improving efficiency and effectiveness in organizations can improve employee engagement and delivery speed of products/services to customers. By improving efficiency, all the above numbers will decrease dramatically, usually by as much as 20% the first time through the process. But it's not all about the process.

Being a Lean organization means much more than being efficient and effective. The organization is healthy, responsive, focused, and transforming. A Lean organization exudes power and is not merely a set of tools and techniques. But getting to power is impossible without the baseline tools and techniques to support the organization. It's like trying to boil the ocean without any heat.

The Fast Track to Change

Here's a hypothetical situation. Company A has been experiencing dropped calls in its customer service department. This situation has led to an increased number of customer complaints. The customer service department's overtime hours are going through the roof to handle this. As you can imagine, this is costing Company A a lot of overtime and lost customers. What should Company A do?

There are two options. They can choose a traditional approach to problem-solving or apply the Kaizen method. Here is how a traditional approach would tackle this problem:

- The organization forms a committee to analyze the situation.

- The committee takes several days or weeks to determine the root cause of the problem (they have several meetings involving all committee members, and someone needs to coordinate all their schedules).

- Once they identify the problem, the committee will reconvene to determine how to correct it. They will propose and agree upon recommendations.

- The committee will then present its recommendations to management for a decision.

- They may draft an implementation plan.

- An implementation committee will implement changes.

- Management will advise employees of the changes and expect employees to adapt.

Now, let's look at how the Kaizen method would solve the problem:

- The organization forms a multidisciplinary team (from across the organization) to analyze the situation.

- A Lean-certified member (and others) gathers data about the problem.

- The team meets over five days to review the data, conduct its analysis, make decisions, prepare an implementation plan, and assign an implementation team leader to effect the changes.

- Since the team is multidisciplinary, adapting to change is seamless: They started their involvement in the project from the start.

There are two critical differences between these two methods. First, the traditional method can take several weeks to months to implement change, whereas the Kaizen method sees change implemented within days to weeks. The second key difference is in change sustainability.

In the traditional method, the process is typically closed-door operations until the committee determines a solution, and only during (or after) implementation does management inform or involve employees. The organization involves employees in the Kaizen event from the start, so change is much easier to sustain.

If you were Company A, which method of problem-solving would you choose?

Managing Inventories

Good inventory management is essential for successful operations. Inventory is any idle material, part, or product an organization keeps in its warehouse or stockroom. Too much inventory usurps a company's cash, space, and employee resources, while too little can result in lost business. Thus, inventory takes up floor space and, as an unsold good, could end up as wasted money.

A typical organization usually has approximately half its current assets in inventory and the other half in receivables and cash. Since inventory could represent a significant portion of total assets in the company's balance sheet, reducing inventory could significantly increase the organization's return on investments. Ultimately, it's in the company's best interest to reduce its inventory while ensuring it has available inventory to meet customer demand.

Organizations can do a few things to reduce their inventory without reducing customer service. For instance, organizations can address the purpose of holding stock in the first place. For example, if merchandise is in transit, the company can locate nearby companies in the supply chain to reduce transit time or ask the manufacturer to drop ship directly to consumers, thus reducing transit time.

Another option for reducing inventory is to ensure good long-term relationships with suppliers and customers and high-quality material. In doing so, the organization has less need for safety inventory (those "just in case the customer needs it, but I don't have it" moments). Thus, with good supplier relationships, the organization does not need to hold inventory.

Reducing ordering and set-up times for inventory and developing sources of supply and demand to cover seasonal ordering are other ways to reduce inventories and increase profits. Cross-training workers is another way. By cross-training workers, the company expands its employee skill sets, increasing flexibility within the organization. Therefore, the company does not need to rely on one individual to do all the inventory ordering and management if that individual happens to be away for a long time. Having everyone better understand how the business operates benefits the organization at all levels.

Finally, keeping inventory manageable means maintaining steady prices and not using sales promotions.

Perfecting Products Before or After Launch

In the realm of efficiency and productivity, clients sometimes ask me about product development. Specifically, is it better to perfect products before launch or launch the product faster and then perfect it when it's already in the market? I will answer this question by referencing Six Sigma practices (the brother of Lean).

Six Sigma aims to have about 99.99 percent of products or services that are free of defects. This goal translates to about 3.4 defects per million and, therefore, a perfect output. You can see then that the goal is near perfection. However, perfection can be costly if the organization's aim is perfection, but its customers would be happy with near perfection. This discrepancy puts the question of perfecting products before or after launch right into the customer's lap.

If your organization is developing products for the market, your organization needs to answer the question, "How well does our process output meet our customer requirements?" Also, is the organization's definition of perfection in line with Six Sigma's definition concerning defects?

An organization that launches a product that does not meet its customers' requirements is setting itself up for failure. For example, if you've developed a new software application but haven't cleaned up major bugs, your customers will not be happy because you have not met their basic requirements concerning the product. You can imagine that there will be several outcomes from this launch. First, your customers are not happy. Second, your customers will go to your competitors. Third, if your competitors' products are better, there's a good chance you've lost your customers forever. Fourth, your organization will lose money. And the list goes on.

But here's another way to look at this example. Where Six Sigma calls for near perfection, the 80/20 Rule tells us to focus on only 20 percent of the product's features that will deliver 80 percent of the requirements. So, the question becomes, "How critical is it to your customer that your product or service be perfect before launch?"

If you're launching a software application that monitors patient breathing, holding off until the product is perfect before launch makes sense. But if you're launching a new game application, focusing on perfecting the critical 20 percent that will control 80 percent of the game's features is perfectly good. Therefore, whether you perfect your product or service before launching or launching it faster and then perfecting depends on your customers' requirements and needs, not the least of which is the product or service criticality.

If you're unsure, put yourself in your customers' shoes. What would you expect from your organization and its products and services if you were the customer?

Understanding What Causes Problems

When reviewing problems, how do you best understand their cause? This question relates to identifying a root cause and is a critical step in understanding how to resolve issues. For instance, if you don't know the problem's root cause, it is unlikely that you will determine the correct problem.

Here's my five-step methodology for identifying the root causes of problems.

1. State the problem. This step is essential so you and your organization understand the project's scope (or the problem, as the case may be).

2. Collect data. One of the best ways to collect data is to conduct interviews with those directly experiencing the problem and those indirectly impacted by the problem. Also, sometimes running focus groups helps bring to light hidden symptoms. For focus groups, ask two questions: 1) What is working well, and 2) What could be improved? Both questions will identify symptoms that you can use to uncover root causes. When conducting one-on-one interviews, use a standard questionnaire to

zero in on root causes. Develop the questionnaire to suit the target program.

3. Observe problems. Sometimes, firsthand experience can be beneficial to understand what is causing problems.

4. Develop an issues template. Use the data collected through interviews, observations, and other means (for example, you may also have created a flowchart of the process) and put your data in an issues template.

The issues template should include the following headings: issue, resolutions, possible causes, and other relationships and impacts. Let's work through an example of an organization experiencing overall records management inefficiencies. (This problem is the stated problem out of which you might identify many issues).

For example, let's look at the issue of inconsistent filing standards as one symptom that stems from overall records management inefficiencies.

- What is the issue? The issue is inconsistent filing standards.

- Next, review and evaluate your data and think about possible causes for the issue. Contributing factors might include that the organization has no records management procedures, staff has no training in records management, the task is not in any job descriptions, no records manager to provide consistent filing standards, etc.

- Now, think about other relationships and the impacts the issue may have on the organization. These could include staff time and productivity loss due to searching through files in different offices, duplicated files within and between offices, and more space required for hardcopy and electronic files. All these relationships and issues result in more cost and less productivity across the organization. I trust this explanation demonstrates how to determine relationships and impacts concerning the matter.

- Finally, conduct a gap analysis based on your data and complete the resolutions column. Solutions to the issue may include writing procedures on how to file, training staff in records management practices, reviewing and ensuring job descriptions include an entry for document filing, assigning a records manager to be responsible for records management, etc.

5. Identify critical issues. Once you complete your issues template, use it to pare down all the issues to the few critical ones. When identifying critical issues, group the problems from the issues template into broader categories.

The critical issues worksheet should contain the following headings: Critical issue, How is the problem manifested, Why is it happening (causes), and Why is it important/its implications?

Following the example of records management inefficiencies and inconsistent filing standards, here is how you might present one critical issue:

- Critical issue – file integrity

- How is the issue manifested? – different classification coding used by different departments, duplication of records across all media, electronic directory structures are not standard and out of control, no document version control, etc.

- Why is the issue happening? – the organization does not have a standard records classification system, policy, procedures, trained staff, naming conventions for electronic files, etc.

- Why is it important? – Incomplete or incorrect documents may be used to make crucial decisions, and fragmented and duplicated files will continue to perpetuate, increasing storage costs (onsite and offsite), increased labor costs to maintain records, public accountability, legal risks, etc.

You could conduct other analyses from here to narrow the problem's resolutions.

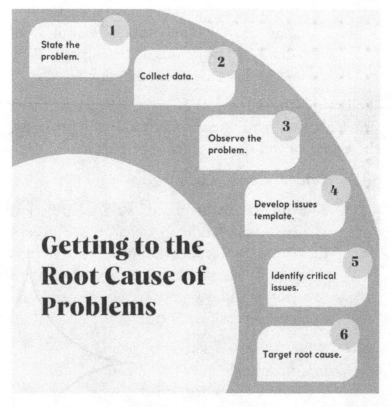

State the problem. **1**

Collect data. **2**

Observe the problem. **3**

Develop issues template. **4**

Getting to the Root Cause of Problems

Identify critical issues. **5**

Target root cause. **6**

However, with the issues template and critical issues analysis, you now understand what is causing the problem. Once you know the cause, your next step is identifying the action(s) that will resolve the problem. Rest assured that with your critical issues identified, you're on the road to recovering efficiency and productivity for your organization.

Service – Now!

When you're in line waiting for service, how long is too long?

Studies show that, on average, waiting more than three minutes is too long. What about customers who stay more than three minutes? There is a strong likelihood that they are dealing with the only available service provider. If customers have choices, they will leave. This statistic is not good news for service providers.

How good is your company at providing top-notch customer service? An online customer service rating company found that DisneyStore.com ranked among the top ten for speediest e-mail support (1 hour, 47 minutes, 40 seconds) and phone support (12 seconds).[17]

In addition to speed (or time), customers are also looking for the following qualities in service.[18]

1. Timeliness. Is the service completed on time? For example, is an overnight package delivered overnight?

2. Completeness. Is everything the customer asked for provided? For example, is an online order complete when delivered?

3. Courtesy. How do employees treat customers? For example, are your company's phone operators professional, and are their voices pleasant?

4. Consistency. Does your company provide the same level of service to each customer each time? For example, if you're still receiving the news in paper format, is your newspaper delivered on time every morning?

5. Accessibility and convenience. How easy is it to obtain the service? For example, when you call The Bay, does the service representative answer quickly?

6. Accuracy. Is the service performed right every time? For example, is your bank or credit card statement correct every month?

7. Responsiveness. How well does the company react to unusual situations (which can happen frequently in a service company)? For example, how well can a telephone operator at Amazon respond to a customer's questions about an online item?

When working with customers, service providers are in a more precarious situation than producers of manufactured goods. Because service can be intangible (unlike a product), it is sometimes hard to know a customer's expectations. A service's fitness for use is often in the eyes of the customer.

By building quality into every dimension of service, organizations will attain service excellence and have happy and loyal customers. All this equates to a healthy bottom line.

Cutting Costs and Optimizing Spend in Small and Mid-size Enterprises

According to Statistics Canada, small and mid-size enterprises (SMEs) are significant contributors to the Canadian economy. In 2021, small businesses comprised over 98 percent of all employers in Canada, employing 10.3 million individuals – almost 63.8 percent of the total labor force. In contrast, medium-sized companies employed 3.4 million individuals, 21.1 percent of the labor force. Large enterprises comprise 15.1 percent of the labor force, employing 2.4 million people. These numbers mean that small and medium-sized businesses have a significant role in the Canadian economy, especially in the post-pandemic era as we drive toward economic recovery.

With this critical economic role, should SMEs consider cutting costs or optimizing spending to improve their cash flow?

First, cutting costs involves reducing the organization's administrative and operational expenses to save money. For instance, reducing staff or purchasing cheaper materials can help companies save money. However, it's essential to consider the trade-offs. Fewer staff members might lead to less responsive customer service while opting for less expensive materials could result in lower-quality products. Both approaches can harm the business in the long term.

Second, optimizing spending by paying less for all business purchases will result in less cost to the business overall. However, if paying less means obtaining poorer quality materials, it is not the best choice. In other words, lesser-quality materials result in inferior products, ultimately impacting customer value. If your customer is no longer receiving the same or better quality product or service from your business, your business is at risk of losing customers.

Depending on the business of the SME, either approach could work short-term, but instead of doing either, why not consider Lean accounting? Let me explain what I mean.

When a business has low cash flow, there can be a knee-jerk reaction to stop spending, but if the process behind the expenditure does not change, SMEs could endure a vicious cycle of spend, overspend, stop spending, and repeat. However, if SMEs control their financial resources based on value streams, they will be better able to reduce business cost pressures. Therefore, using Lean accounting is the way to go.

In traditional cost accounting, businesses categorize expenses by department. On the other hand, in Lean accounting, the organization uses value streams. By allocating costs to value streams—the flow of activities required to transform raw materials or information into a product or service for customer use—the business has a better way of capturing the performance of its operations.

An organization practicing Lean principles focuses on eliminating waste and only producing to meet customer demand. It also bases its work on value streams. In addition, Lean companies boost their inventory turnover and reduce inventory levels (in all aspects – administration and operations). They focus on achieving the shortest possible production cycle to meet customer demand. The benefits include lower production costs, higher product quality (because the company only produces to meet the customer demand; there is no guessing and "just in case" supply), and shorter lead times.

Implementing Lean in SMEs often leads to its financial statements showing a temporary hit to the bottom line as their deferred labor and overhead move from the inventory account on the balance sheet to the expense section of the income statement. In other words, the company's financial statements may not reflect the actual benefits of its Lean process.

Therefore, there is a dichotomy in actual vs. reported performance—chartered professional accountants (CPAs) want to account for finances in a Lean company accurately, but they also don't want to report the company as not profitable. For example, one of the issues with Lean manufacturing is that instead of sharing equipment across the organization, Lean processes operate in work cells where everything needed to manufacture a part is in the sequence required for the part.

Think about it this way. In a traditional organization, manufacturing a specific product might take about four months because parts might move through a dozen or more operations across the factory flow. The company would thus keep large parts inventories while assemblies sit idle, waiting to move to the next step. This approach wastes space, and machines require frequent maintenance because they constantly move between steps.

However, a Lean company creates work cells for each product it produces. Therefore, instead of moving the required machines to build the part, the company locates the required devices together within a work cell in the production sequence, all in one place.

In addition, the work cells include worker cross-training to perform various operations. Another great benefit is that the company orders supplies for that product in that work cell when required. As a result, companies can reduce their production time from months to hours.

Now, let's go back to the traditional cost accounting method. If SMEs use traditional cost accounting, they use a system designed to support mass production, i.e., typically in large organizations. In addition, traditional cost accounting reports intend to inform outsiders, not provide an accurate accounting of the organization's process(es). Lean accounting is much better at capturing the organization's performance of operations.

As a company transforms from traditional mass production to Lean production (going from extensive inventories moved across the entire floor to smaller inventories stationed within work cells), how the company counts, controls, and measures will change. Also, standard cost accounting was developed in the early 1900s when most companies' structures consisted of 60 percent direct labor, 30 percent materials, and 10 percent overhead.[19] Today, the percentages differ, with direct labor accounting for between five and 15 percent.

In addition, inventory is not an asset since it incurs handling costs, takes up floor space, and reduces cash flow (Lean employs the just-in-time inventory concept to reduce inventory). Where traditional accounting might overvalue inventory because of an assumption that it will sell at market price, this is not the case. Lean adherents will tell you that products stocked in inventory sooner become obsolete than achieve a sale, and if they do sell, it is for less than market value.

Lean accounting is not a panacea but is better for tracking value stream costs and revenues. However, if practiced too rigorously, a Lean approach might emphasize speed and quality (what customers want) to exclude cost concerns (the SME still wants to stay in the black!). For example, machine shops that produce widgets could have up to several days lead times if they don't use Lean concepts.

On the other hand, employees can cut lead times from days to hours with Lean by simply reorganizing and better scheduling their work. Then, the company can cut lead times even further to minutes if the organization invests in new machinery. In other words, faster isn't always better because there is a cost involved.

I hope I have convinced you that SMEs following a Lean approach using a Lean cost accounting method would be in a much better position to understand their operation's profit and loss rather than deciding between cost cutting or optimizing spending.

Realistically, cost cutting (e.g., reaction to overspending or poor sales) and optimizing spending (e.g., using Lean systems) are built into the Lean approach because the company would treat each process line (or value stream) separately. Lean accounting creates more straightforward and easier-to-follow reporting methods, which provide SMEs with more efficient and accurate cost tracking.

The Root of Airport Delays and Flight Cancellations

In the summer of 2022, perhaps like many, I followed the state of our nation's flight delays and cancellations with interest. However, my particular interest is that I was on vacation and wanted to return home to Canada. Several articles from the CBC, CTV, The Wall Street Journal, and others succinctly indicated that processing passengers through airport terminals and customs directly results from staffing shortages. Others pointed to greedy airlines wanting to recoup their pandemic losses by over-scheduling flights – the nerve, right?!

I like to travel, although I don't particularly appreciate flying. I have traveled annually or more often for over 20 years. About a decade ago, I traveled through Toronto. Given Toronto's dubious honor today as being the worst airport in the world for flight delays and cancellations.[20]

A decade ago, it took us over an hour to clear customs in Toronto, resulting in a missed Air Canada flight. In our frustration, we didn't accept the airport's offer to overnight and catch another flight in the morning. Instead, we got our bags and booked a flight with WestJet that evening to get home after a long international flight. That was then. Now, the media are reporting even worse lineups at Toronto's Pearson Airport.

The Los Angeles Times[21] stated that the number of complaints about airline services jumped 237% in May 2022 compared to May 2019. The analytics company that compiled the research indicated that perhaps the decline in satisfaction was due to airlines' inability to manage the increased travel demands. Perhaps. However, in the Toronto case, CBC News[22] reported that the number of foreign arrivals to Canada by air in June 2022 (and thus the need to clear customs) decreased by about one-third compared to June 2019. Therefore, can we assume that non-foreign travel increased through Toronto's customs? Unfortunately, the article did not elaborate.

CTV News[23] noted that Canada's Transport Minister stated that many European airports also struggled with delays and long lines, sometimes stretching outside the terminal. However, neither CTV nor the Minister provided an example. We traveled through the United States, Germany, and Croatia in 2022. We experienced no long delays or cancellations. Life felt normal.

News media also reported that airports are committed to hiring more staff to get passengers through the terminal faster; however, this solution is surely missing the point. Throwing more staff into a flawed process creates more of the same; only this time, more staff are trying to navigate a bad system, which will add a burden to the system.

In Lean operations, the first thing that an organization asks is, "What does my customer want from me/my business?" In the airline industry—let's look at the airport terminal because that's where the congestion happens—the airport should ask the same thing: "What do passengers want from this terminal?" The answer: The customer wants speedy processing without undue delays and no flight cancellations.

Now, let's look at Toronto. What is Toronto doing to earn the top spot as the worst airport in the world? Well, what it is not doing is asking the crucial question. If it had asked, it would know the answer. First, the world has all but quashed pandemic measures, but Canada seems reluctant to let go of the ArriveCan app.

We used that app last year upon return to Canada since it was mandatory, and we didn't know how to avoid it; from that experience, I can confirm the app did nothing to expedite me through customs – i.e., it did nothing to help me, the customer. Then I asked how it is helping Canada. I will leave that an open question for your consideration. Looking at it more broadly, how is this app assisting the taxpayer (remember, whatever the government spends, it's your money; the government has no money)?

Second, how will hiring more border security staff in Toronto (and/or other airports) solve the problem of a flawed process bloated by an unnecessary application (e.g., ArriveCan) that does not serve the passenger?

Third, why is the terminal short-staffed? What led to the staffing issues, and were those decisions relating to staff downsizing in the passengers' best interests? I suggest that staff downsizing was a short-sighted decision in many businesses.

Fourth, how are airlines contributing to the problem? What could they do/have done better to ease the pain at airport terminals? Blaming airlines for over-scheduling is a cop-out. Airlines are doing what they have always done and are keen to improve business, just like passengers are eager to travel like they did pre-pandemic.

Fifth, we could blame the pandemic for all the airport woes, but that is nonsense. Businesses—airports included—need to plan appropriately for any business interruption. Adding bureaucratic layers to the process is never in the passengers' best interest. Bureaucratic layers are typically "non-value-add" elements that do nothing to improve customer service (although many such non-value-add factors detract and slow customer service).

Thus, to make Toronto Pearson Airport a thriving hub of activity and profit, it's time for airport executives to evaluate their operations with the following three questions. (Note that I am using the ArriveCan app as an example, but I'm sure you can think of other areas for improvement like random COVID testing, wearing masks, airplanes waiting on the tarmac and letting passengers out in limited numbers, baggage claims and transfers, information telephone lines that don't get answered, etc.).

1. Does the passenger care about or want the ArriveCan app? In other words, is it serving the passenger (i.e., the customer)?

2. Does the ArriveCan app physically transform the service process through customs for the better (i.e., does it improve the process for the passenger/customer)?

3. Is the ArriveCan fail-proof (i.e., is the product/service done "right the first time" without DOWNTIME for the passenger /customer)?

As the business owner, if you answer "no" to any of the above questions, you have lost sight of the customer/passenger in your business. As a result, your operation is bloated and needs a Lean makeover.

Lean organizations focus on the customer and the value they can deliver to the customer. They do not integrate heavy regulations or rules that hinder customer service. If you don't know what value you provide to your customer, that's another challenge. But look at it this way: An airport with an efficient process can keep its costs down. These costs are tangible (dollars, profit) and intangible (passenger satisfaction, staff morale). On the other hand, inefficient processes incur higher product and service costs.

Customers who value your products or services will pay your asking price. Ultimately, if your service does not meet your passengers' criteria for value, you can bet those passengers will be looking to fly through other airports or countries.

IMPROVE

Kaizen to the Rescue

Successful organizational improvement initiatives depend on successful follow-up and maintenance. To this end, Kaizen is a practical continuous improvement approach, literally translated to "change for the best" or "good change."

Kaizen is a Lean methodology that includes a set of activities applied continuously to all functions in an organization. What sets Kaizen apart from other improvement methodologies is that it involves all employees in the organization—from the CEO to the front-line workers. Also, Kaizen is easy to apply in any organization and to all processes.

A curious element of Kaizen is its ability to disarm the brain's fear response, making change come more naturally. Participants lose their fear of change through gentle guidance, gradual questioning, and process evaluation. This situation opens individuals to possibilities they may not have thought of previously.

Kaizen originates in Japanese businesses, but its influence since the Second World War is worldwide. The reason is simple: Kaizen humanizes the workplace by involving all employees to spot and eliminate waste in business processes. The process is transparent and inclusive of all those involved: suppliers, customers, employees, and other stakeholders.

The continuous improvement from Kaizen is a daily process of evaluating workflow and eliminating waste on the spot. Workflow is slow and wasteful in many organizations bogged down with policies, directives, and other checking mechanisms. But with Kaizen, directly eliminating waste targets these checking mechanisms to improve efficiency and productivity, enabling a faster workflow.

Another benefit of Kaizen is that it usually only delivers minor improvements. Over time, these small improvements accumulate into significant improvements because they involve many (all) processes throughout the organization. This compound productivity improvement means considerable savings in time and money for the organization—systematically replacing inefficient practices with customer value-adding practices is a win–win for all stakeholders.

Kaizen replaces the command-and-control mid-twentieth-century models of improvement programs. Because those who directly work in the process carefully monitor the process changes, Kaizen's continuous improvement is sustainable. In addition, changes are typically on a smaller scale, so monitoring and sustaining long-term gains is easier.

While Kaizen events are usually week-long blitzes of improvement and are limited in scope, issues identified at one event are instrumental in informing subsequent improvement events. This paying-it-forward approach of plan-do-check-act helps maintain a cycle of continuous improvement in all the processes in the organization.

It is interesting, but perhaps not surprising, that Kaizen has evolved into personal development principles because of its simplicity. Check out Robert Maurer's book *One Small Step Can Change Your Life: The Kaizen Way* to learn more about Kaizen and how to apply it in your organization.[24]

Accelerating Project Success

Ahh, the project. Who among us has never had to do one? No matter what line of work you're in, the chances are that you have engaged in projects at one time or another. Anything from planning an event such as a small dinner gathering to building infrastructure like bridges and highways or creating and launching spaceships comes under the purview of a project. But did you know that the amount and quality of project planning largely determines project success?

The *Project Management Body of Knowledge*[25] considers a project plan a formal, approved document that a project manager can use to guide projects from execution to control. However, there are many occasions when such a document may seem over-the-top (e.g., dinner party planning). But no matter the size of the project, having documentation to guide you through execution is a good idea.

Consider this. We can generally trace successful projects to planning work that can take up to 80% of the project manager's (and others') time. What, you ask? When do they have time to execute the plan? You may be surprised to learn that the planning of projects touches nine project knowledge areas,[26] whereas the execution process covers only five areas. Of the five project processes (initiation, planning, execution, control, and closing), only initiation and closing have fewer steps than execution.

How do you make sure you have a foolproof project plan? Here are five considerations:

1. Define the purpose. Why are you doing the project? What is its purpose? If you don't know why, you won't know how to plan for the project. Knowing the goal will help you define what success looks and feels like for the project.

2. Allow freedom to happen, but don't lose control. Identify what needs to be in place (e.g., policies, procedures, standards) to ensure project success. Then, put this in place and trust your project team to move the project forward.

3. Engage your team. Use brainstorming to fill in the gaps in your plan, but before doing so, make sure the team is comfortable with one another to encourage a free flow of ideas. Mind mapping used during brainstorming allows everyone to see the gaps and makes them easier to fill. A picture is worth more than a thousand words.

4. Write the plan. Organize your plan logically so that left- and right-brain people can

glean understanding. Use a simple at-a-glance template and add detail in an appendix. Below is a template that I like. It captures the define-measure-analyze-improve-control (DMAIC) principles of Lean.

5. Make decisions. As you implement your project plan, regularly keep checking the plan. Modify the plan during implementation, as necessary. Remember, plans are just that—plans. They are guides in the process. You can and should adjust the plan to fit the reality of implementation.

Your complete project plan will include assumptions and decisions about the project and the project's estimated (and approved) scope, cost, and schedule. Another advantage of a project plan is that it helps to facilitate communication among stakeholders; they don't need to guess about the project since the plan contains all the details. Thus, you can count these elements toward the successful outcomes of your project!

The project charter worksheet on the next page provides ideas for laying out your document. You might also want to meld this information with an A3 (discussed in *A3 Problem-solving* in this book).

PROJECT CHARTER WORKSHEET

Project Title:

Business Case:

Problem/Opportunity Statement:

Goal Statement:

Project Scope:

Project Champion:	Other Stakeholders:
Project Sponsor:	
Project Manager:	
Steering Committee:	

Estimated Cost Savings:	Realized/Actual Cost Savings: (This will be completed after the project is complete)

Preliminary Plan	Target Date	Actual Date	Notes/Lessons Learned:
Start Date			(This will be completed after the project is complete)
DEFINE			
MEASURE			
ANALYZE			
IMPROVE			
CONTROL			
Completion Date			

TERMINOLOGY:

DEFINE = Map the process, identify the problem (what are we measuring? Who/what is impacted?)

MEASURE = Data collection plan (how will you collect data?)

ANALYZE = Analyze data (effectiveness), process (efficiency), and root cause

IMPROVE = Determine solutions (e.g., brainstorming, affinity diagram, etc.)

CONTROL = Set up control measures (e.g., Audits?)

The #1 Red Light: A Lack of Urgency

There are many reasons why change may stall, but the number one reason is lack of urgency. If the project team lacks urgency toward achieving goals, this behavior should raise immediate alarm for project champions and leaders.

Sometimes, a lack of urgency exists because people don't understand the project's purpose. For example, no one provided clarity around goals and objectives. When this happens, people would rather live with the problem as it currently exists than accept a solution they do not understand. Therefore, project leaders must present a clear business case to motivate staff and instill urgency in the change by demonstrating how the project will improve the organization's condition.

In addition, the organization must build a strong business case and provide extensive training, communicating early and throughout the process. If not, a lack of urgency will persist.

Here are some other ways in which to handle the lack of urgency. First, evaluate the external threats to the organization. These threats may form the basis of a business case to get the project moving and instill urgency. Second, benchmarking is also an effective tool to identify what the organization can do to differentiate itself from the competition. In addition, consider the following approaches.

1. Educate top management to help them understand how the initiative can directly benefit their and their organization's performance. Top-down commitment to the project is essential.

2. Align metrics and goals. Define three to seven primary objectives and how they will improve the organization's condition. If the list is more extensive than this, analysis paralysis may overwhelm employees, and nothing will get done.

3. Regular communication exposes employees to concepts and possibilities of new paradigms and the benefits of doing things differently. Show them, don't just tell them. Use examples from other organizations or small implementations in different parts of your organization.

4. Do a pilot project for a quick hit. The pilot project should provide visible and undeniable evidence of success that employees can see quickly. When they see this, they can visualize future success for the whole company. Along these lines,

people sometimes may need to see why *not* changing will inhibit future success, almost more so than how changing will improve the chances for success.

5. Buffer employees from top management so they can try new things without the executive always saying nay. It's sometimes easier to apologize after the fact rather than ask for permission beforehand. Let employees implement small changes to prove that the concept works for themselves and the organization. By doing so, you can divert some urgency back into the organization.

When the organization has a sense of urgency for change, teams will likely complete projects within the allotted timeframes, and there is also a greater likelihood of sustainable change.

Some experts suggest that urgency should drive change, and change should occur within no more than nine months. So, if you've got a large project, break it out into bite-size pieces where it takes only a few months to complete each piece. By doing this, you will have many successful wins, demonstrating that the organization can achieve long-term success and sustainable change.

The 5S Method

The 5S is a Japanese methodology developed by Taiichi Ohno and Eiji Toyoda, Japanese industrial engineers, in 1950. Given its commonsense approach, it is still an accepted practice today and a fundamental concept in Lean methodology. Each step of the 5S method starts with the letter S, as follows:

1. Sort (Seiri). The sorting process involves reviewing your workspace and distinguishing between what is and is not needed. It's about decluttering your workspace and leaving only critical things you need to succeed. The adage, *when in doubt, move it out*, applies here.

2. Set in order (Seiton). After sorting and decluttering, the next step is to organize everything that remains. Organizing includes making locations visible and self-explanatory and designating storage locations for everything, including tools, incoming and outgoing items, job aides, information sheets, etc. The keys to organizing are visual controls (i.e., well-organized locations allow you to immediately notice if something belongs in that location or is missing), immediate retrieval (e.g., think about color-coded filing systems), and quick return.

3. Shine (Seiso). There are three phases in shining your workspace. First is daily cleanliness, second is cleanliness inspections, and third is cleanliness maintenance. While one might think shining is about cleaning, that's not entirely true since cleaning is about safety and efficiency. Remember the sorting you did in step one? If you don't maintain order, the result becomes chaos.

4. Standardize (Seiketsu). When we standardize our workspace and workflow, we achieve best practices. We do this by developing and implementing 5S checklists to identify what will be done, who is responsible, and when the task needs doing. In addition, we can create a visual workplace through color coding (e.g., use red to indicate a low inventory requiring re-order, green for a good inventory level, and yellow for too much inventory). Visual standards help the organization record problems, where everyone can quickly identify defects. Visual workplaces usually have good 5S practices.

5. Sustain (Shitsuke). After standardizing the workflow, you now must sustain it through standards. Policies and procedures are helpful in this regard, as are audits. However, while starting with 5S in your workspace is excellent, sustaining a good workflow organization-wide requires 5S implementtation throughout the entire organization.

Another thing to consider in improving overall organizational productivity is eliminating excess equipment and inventory. In other words, reduce waste. By removing the excess, the organization will experience fewer equipment breakdowns, longer equipment life, fewer defects and higher quality, and more efficient and effective operations. Eliminating excess equipment and inventory also saves time and cost and makes the workplace easier to maintain and improve production schedules, reducing motion and waste. Ultimately, a visual workplace is critical to streamlined workflow.

Here is a snapshot of 5S to help you get started toward reducing waste in your workspace and organization.

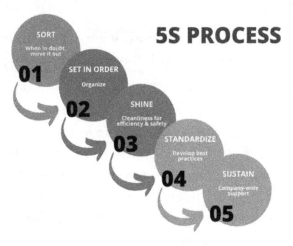

5S PROCESS

SORT
When in doubt, move it out
01

SET IN ORDER
Organize
02

SHINE
Cleanliness for efficiency & safety
03

STANDARDIZE
Develop best practices
04

SUSTAIN
Company-wide support
05

The People Problem

Much research is on good and bad leadership and how good leaders build and promote thriving organizations while bad leaders quickly quash progress. I recently had an experience with bad leadership (*really bad* leadership) and saw firsthand how the organization's people—the very assets organizations hold dear—made bad leadership worse. While poor leadership is one thing (and there are ways to manage this issue), the organization's assets—its people—can sometimes do more damage to the organization than its inept leaders.

In an organization where I was recently involved, here is what I observed about its people:

1. Complacency. Those who are complacent don't care about what happens to the organization. They believe their life is good and can't see outside their shells to notice the organization struggling. They don't care about making a positive difference in the organization; they are content to keep the wheels turning just as they are and just for themselves.

2. Self-interest. Like the complacent, those with self-interests will never speak up on behalf of the entire organization. These people only care about themselves. They will sit on the sidelines instead of speaking up or even side with the bad leader if it serves their interest. Those who work for their self-interest are not individuals in whom one could place any trust for the benefit of the entire organization.

3. Fear. Those afraid of rocking the boat are another problem in the organization. For whatever reason (perhaps fear of change or losing their jobs), those who fear speaking up may stand behind someone who will speak for them; they don't particularly care where they're standing. However, when it's their turn to speak, they never do. These people grumble, but not when it matters or to whom it matters.

4. Incompetence. Sadly, any organization has incompetent people (starting from the leader and downward). The incompetent will try to sound smart, but one can easily see through their veils. Sadly, an incompetent leader's b**s*** can dupe many people.

5. Talker. The long-winded gas bags take up too much time, and even if they say

something useful in the end, because they talk so long, people lose interest in listening to them. If they expect others to take them seriously, gasbags must learn to reach a meaningful point quickly.

6. Inability to walk the talk. These individuals spout off many things that need fixing in the organization, but when it comes time to fulfill their promises and get things done, they do not follow through. Eventually, others realize these people are full of hot air and can't be relied upon for positive organizational change.

The bottom line is that while people are necessary for an efficient organization, the type of people that make up an organization is as important as the type of leaders. One cannot overstress quality over quantity.

I learned from my experience in this organization that one person can't make a change. One person can initiate change, but if the organization's people don't support the difference, then change will not happen.

Organizations need exceptional leaders for success, but people are just as important. Without the right mix of leadership and culture, organizational progress is impossible.

That's The Way We Do It Here

Culture includes specific behaviors acquired (partly) from social influences. These social influences can come from family, friends, co-workers, and others. When we wish to focus on efficiency improvement, culture can be an aid or a hindrance, depending on whether the culture is affected by forces encouraging or resisting change. Let me give you a couple of examples.

A prominent public sector director told me his company's processes generally worked well because staff regularly engaged in process improvement activities. I asked how his company knew what methods needed improving. It turns out they don't know. Instead, they tweak here and there without looking at the big picture and never consider the process's value to the customer. When I suggested that culture may be a factor, he said he didn't think they had an issue with change resistance and that they've always done things this way.

During a meeting with another executive leader, I learned that his department held the belief that one could not improve processes in the services industry. "We're not in manufacturing; we're already doing the most work possible with our limited resources." I gave him examples of process inefficiencies in service industries, such as multiple approvals on documents, loss of time due to waiting for work, inadequate computer systems that contribute to errors and waiting time, vague forms, or duplicated information across multiple documents, etc. He agreed that this could occur in his organization, but he didn't believe the impact on work was enormous. "We can't improve any more – we're already stretched."

In both instances, organizational culture hinders change, and the organization's leaders are its main adversaries. Successful change initiatives receive support from the top. These companies are stuck in a status quo paradigm. However, the news is not all bad. Staff can stir change.

Unhappy workers, high turnover, multiple re-dos of work products, systems that crash, extensive downtime, and other inopportunities can help an organization's leaders to start thinking differently about how they do things. Staff and customers can perpetuate conflict by asking questions about why the organization does things a certain way until the organization finds a definitive answer (or what generally happens, there is no definitive answer, which forces leaders into action).

Another way to produce change is through technology. However, the danger of applying technology to pre-existing processes is that inefficient processes spur organizational inefficiency. The upside (if one can call this an upside) is that increasing inefficiencies will eventually grind operations to a halt. Leaders will then have to take notice.

One simple yet effective way to invoke change is through an employee suggestion program. A quality culture focused on continuous improvement will implement at least 90 percent of its employees' suggestions. Consider this: at one point, Toyota received 75,000 tips from 7,000 employees and implemented 99 percent of those suggestions. This approach is one of the things that makes Toyota a leader in productivity.

If you're a leader content with hiding behind "that's the way we do it here," it may be time to re-examine your beliefs. Change your thoughts to change your organization's culture to become a culture of continuous improvement. Doing so will significantly benefit the organization due to improved productivity, quality, safety, speedier delivery, lower costs, and greater customer satisfaction.

How Organizations Can Identify Areas for Improvement

Typically, organizations will identify a problem and then work to identify the root cause of the problem to come up with a solution for implementation. But what if there are several, few, or no issues in the organization, but you would like to improve your organization? How do you go about identifying areas for improvement? One of the best ways I know how an organization can identify areas for improvement is to use a Lean assessment methodology.

The Lean assessment helps an organization identify potential opportunities for improvement at a high level and provides an understanding of the process before a change occurs. It is a systematic evaluation that documents the current state of the business and what the business can expect in the future. Typical areas evaluated through a Lean assessment include the company's current culture, market expectations, customer satisfaction, employee skills requirements, readiness to change, and others that management might identify. Ultimately, you can evaluate any area. Here are the steps to performing a Lean assessment in your organization:

1. Meetings. Meet with key and controlling stakeholders to determine expectations and timelines for the Lean assessment.

2. Determine the project scope. Write a project charter to contain the project.

3. Conduct interviews with staff to gather answers to specific questions. What are the perceived levels of empowerment in the business? There is value in speaking to as many staff as possible to identify the business's strengths, weaknesses, opportunities, and threats. Also include other situational topics specific to your business.

4. Develop benchmarking for several areas in your organization. For example, include strategic and operational planning in your review, workplace organization, IT systems, human resources development, current accounting practices, operational performance, sales and marketing, and other areas that you feel could or should be included in the assessment.

5. Prepare summary and detailed reports of your findings and include specific areas for initial improvement, reasons, and possible solutions. Estimate the amount of internal and external resources and provide high-level recommendations from your results.

6. Meet with the key and controlling stakeholders to present your findings and recommendations and determine steps forward.

But what should a company do now that you have all this information? Initially, start with a minimally intrusive area, such as corporate culture or readiness for change. Then, get stakeholder buy-in for change in that area. Your initial efforts should include a full-scale investigation in the area that you have chosen, as well as extensive benchmarking as you establish your go-forward plan.

Whatever area you choose and however you choose to implement change, a crucial ingredient is and will be people. Include as many people from your organization as possible in the project early in the planning stage to capture and hear their ideas. Nothing is worse than initiating and implementing a project solo because you don't want to make waves for staff. You need to make waves. You need to get staff involved. The more involved they are, the more accepting they will be of the change. Also, it will be much easier to implement the changes during the project if you involve staff early.

Ultimately, identifying areas for improvement in an organization depends on what areas you choose to study and evaluate and what areas stakeholders agree as priorities—those areas that, once improved, will markedly improve the organization's performance and bottom line.

Don't forget: no matter how you proceed, document your lessons learned so that subsequent projects can be even better.

Secrets to Project Success

Perhaps the best way to define project success is to provide reasons for failure. Five areas generally lead to project success or failure.

First is team dynamics. A team that cannot work well together will inevitably not create solid project plans or deliver project tasks on time or with quality. Thus, having a team charter in place will help establish a focus for the team, motivate their behavior, and guide their collaboration on projects. On the other hand, a project charter will help the team get over plateaus because the project charter lists requirements for specific projects.

Second is scope creep. The project scope defines the boundaries of the project work. Scope creep occurs when what is outside the project's scope seeps into what is inside the project, expanding the project scope to which the team did not agree. Thus, precisely defining the project scope is essential to ensure the project stays on track.

Third is project scope. If the organization based the project scope on poor or no root causation, the project is merely working on correcting symptoms rather than the cause of the problem. One cannot claim project success when one corrects only symptoms because the problem persists. In addition, a poorly defined project scope can lead to scope creep (see the previous paragraph). The scope determines the project's goals, constraints, strategies, tasks, and deliverables.

Fourth relates to no project champion. A project champion is essential to a project's success since the champion is the one who allocates the resources for the project (including money, people, time, equipment, etc.) and removes the project's roadblocks. Without a champion, it isn't easy to progress. The champion has an informal role in the project, providing inspirational and motivational support to team members. The champion is the project's advocate and ensures project stakeholders are satisfied.

Fifth refers to no stakeholder buy-in. Stakeholders are critical to a project's success. They help the company meet its strategic objectives by contributing their experiences and perspectives to a project. They can also provide the necessary materials and resources. Their support is crucial to a successful project.

A well-defined project scope can alleviate the top five reasons for project derailment since it will help galvanize a project team, its champion, and stakeholders.

Top Ways to Improve Team Dynamics on a Project

If you're working on a project, you're most likely working with a team, and you know that sometimes there can be conflict within teams. The differences and similarities people bring to the team can influence the team's dynamics. So, how do you improve team dynamics to maximize high performance?

Fundamentally, teams change how members relate to each other, the organization, and management. People assigned to teams are empowered; they are set free, and it's difficult to cage up teams, so you can see how teams can become entities unto themselves. The elements of a good team include:

- They are goal-driven.

- They share objectives.

- They operate in a climate of trust and openness.

- They have a sense of belonging to the team.

- They value diversity.

- They feel encouraged to be creative and take risks.

- They meet the goals of the project.

With these elements, appropriate project timelines, and funding, teams can be outstanding performers. However, sometimes, teams run into roadblocks and cannot identify the need for change. According to Dee Hock,[27] the problem isn't about thinking up new ideas but how to get the old ideas out. To demonstrate this, fold your hands in a prayer position. Notice which thumb is on top. Now, try the prayer position with your other thumb on top. How does this feel? If you're like most people, this feels unusual, perhaps even uncomfortable. Now, imagine trying to implement a change across your organization.

Your team's task is to implement change, but in doing so, they must convince themselves that this change is necessary before they can energetically work on the project. Thus, the team's different modes of thinking will influence their dynamics. The secret to improving team dynamics is helping the team switch from intuitive (or traditional) thinking to counterintuitive (or long-term) thinking. The best way to do this is to understand each team member's behavioral style and what makes them tick.

One way to understand their style is through an inventory of personal types, such as the Myers Briggs Inventory (MBI) or a True Colors inventory. By having this inventory beforehand, you, as the project leader/manager, will understand how to engage your team members best. For instance, in the True Colors, those who score predominantly red are known as adventurers, those with green are planners, the brown color is mostly a builder, and the blue color is a relater. Let me demonstrate this.

Red team members. These are problem solvers who need opportunities to perform. They also need praise for their achievements and recognition for their performance. How do you motivate Reds? Give them more challenges, another chance to be in the middle of the problem so that they can demonstrate their skill.

Green team members. These people need structure, and they need to know the purpose of their work. Involve them in decision-making and praise their insights. They work best within assigned boundaries.

Brown team members. These individuals are practical and conservative; their strength is knowing what they want and need to do. However, they can steamroll others to get there. Handle Browns by giving them consistent feedback and letting them organize things. Reward them with public recognition.

Blue team members. These are the "emotional" people. They don't like conflict and appear to be loners to others. The best way to work with Blue team members is through personal contact. Also, they like small talk to indicate that you are interested in them first.

Ultimately, your team needs each behavioral style type to succeed: Reds, Greens, Browns, and Blues. Build your team by spending time with each of them one-on-one to get them to trust you and learn about each member and their behavior. Knowing their behavior style will help you relate to them more effectively. This personal touch will create a positive team dynamic and enable your project to be successful.

Using Internal Resources to Implement Projects

An organization can use its internal resources to implement new projects even if internal resources are not subject matter experts (SMEs). Here's how: have your staff work alongside SMEs to learn how to implement projects in one or more pilot sites. By working alongside SMEs, staff learn detailed implementation procedures, which procedures they can apply to other sites as implementation progresses. This approach sounds simple, and it is, but there are a few considerations for using this approach.

1. Ensure that staff working with SMEs have the delegated authority and responsibility for this aspect of the program upon completion of implementation. For instance, it would not make economic or strategic sense to assign one staff member to work with the SME and another to manage the program after implementation if the assigned staff has no expertise in the program area.

2. The organization must give staff working with SMEs the necessary time to work on

the project. Therefore, other staff will need to cover the work usually done by staff. Those working with SMEs must feel confident and not pressured to perform dual roles during the project.

3. The organization must pay fair compensation to staff working with SMEs. This compensation may require a review and revision of existing job descriptions.

4. Selected staff must not be "voluntold" to work on the project. Recruiting interested staff with skills in the new program is a much better approach. If staff is interested in the program, they will be amenable to learning new skills that will carry forward to program maintenance after project completion.

5. Don't assume that upon pilot project completion, the staff who worked alongside the SME are now experts in the subject matter if they weren't experts before. They will still need support and guidance from the SME and the organization as they continue to learn how to manage the program.

During implementation, issues will arise requiring input from the project manager, project team members, and staff within the project implementation areas. By involving staff early, they gradually learn about the program and will be more comfortable and knowledgeable about its application when the project is complete. It makes long-term strategic and economic sense to involve staff during the implementation of projects, even if they are not experts in the subject matter.

Best Practices for Effective Implementation Plans

People often ask me about best practices for effective implementation plans. Their question is good since implementation plans are crucial to any program. If there is incorrect implementation, the program does not meet its intent. In addition, other unintended consequences, such as decreased staff morale and project participation and increased costs, can stop the program entirely. So, what must one do to ensure effective implementation and implementation plans?

Here are the ten requirements that I always consider for successful program implementation. These requirements are the foundation of implementation plans.

1. Business readiness. Before implementation can begin in any organization area, that area must be ready to accept the new program. A business readiness checklist helps determine business readiness.

2. Liaison roles. One staff member must oversee the implementation in their area. Whether they manage the implementation or work with a consultant during the implementation, the staff liaison will be the

go-to person for other staff. This staff liaison will understand the program firsthand by participating in the implementation.

3. Software or other equipment. Identify and ensure that all software or other equipment and supplies are onsite at the required time for starting implementation in the business unit.

4. Training. Ensure that all business units receive introductory training before implementation begins and full training after implementation completion.

5. Communication. Prepare and follow a communication plan during the implementation project.

6. Scheduling. Managing an effective schedule is essential for ensuring appropriate staff involvement at the correct time. In addition, scheduling the entire implementation project is vital for overall project management.

7. Resources. Ensure that you itemize and have available all resources required for the implementation project.

8. Logistics. Someone needs to oversee logistics for the project. Ensure the appropriate management of all goods and services orders and deliveries.

9. Budget. Money is a crucial element of any project, especially implementation. Ensure you have estimated the implementation cost and that funding is available for the entire project.

10. Change management. Before, during, and after implementation, a change management strategy must be in place to help you deal with the changes resulting from implementation. A change management plan can help you deal with the challenges of change.

With these ten considerations for successful project implementation, write the project charter for your plan.

There you have it. All you need now is to get working on developing your project implementation plan and then, of course, implementing your plan.

Remember that even though you may have perfected the plan and implementation is well underway, change is the only constant of our times. Be prepared to accept new and better solutions at any point during or after implementation. The graphic below summarizes my steps for "no-fail" implementation plans.

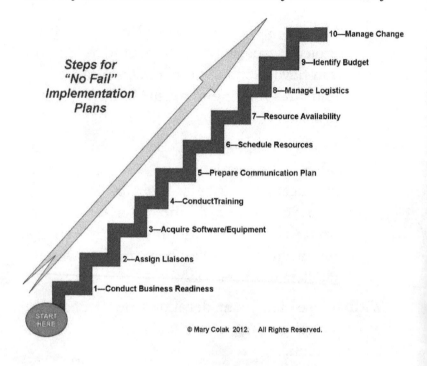

Steps for "No Fail" Implementation Plans

10—Manage Change
9—Identify Budget
8—Manage Logistics
7—Resource Availability
6—Schedule Resources
5—Prepare Communication Plan
4—ConductTraining
3—Acquire Software/Equipment
2—Assign Liaisons
1—Conduct Business Readiness

START HERE

The Productivity Mindset

When I first visited Croatia in the 1970s, I immediately noticed retail workers' negative attitudes and reluctance to assist customers. I remember entering one shop where I wasn't allowed to touch the merchandise, and I felt like I was bothering the sales clerk when I asked for assistance. I quickly exited.

Years later, I reflect on this earlier experience and compare it to my recent visits. What a difference a democracy and a free market make! In the 1970s, Croatia had a communist regime, but today, its government is learning and applying democratic principles. The change in worker attitudes is unmistakably positive. This trickle-down effect can apply at any level, macro or micro, such as at the corporate level, literally anywhere there are leaders and followers.

Imagine working in an environment that does not encourage innovation, is change averse, and does nothing to reward employees for extra effort. If you are an employee in this environment, what is your attitude? It may very well be negative and perhaps obstructionist. Because your organization does not give you the tools and experiences to flourish, you might compare your organization's operations with those of a Third World country.

While it is true that we, as individuals, can choose to have a positive or negative attitude, employers are responsible for providing an environment that encourages positive attitudes. However, this does not admonish the individual. It is simple to blame our employer for our negative attitudes, but we must also consider that we have a choice. We can choose to be positive or negative, no matter our circumstances.

Some psychological studies suggest that negative attitudes may prevail when one is dissatisfied with one's lot in life, leading to resentment of anyone else getting ahead. A resentful person in the workplace may exhibit behaviors such as not getting things done on time, not being helpful to others, not freely offering information that they know can save time, etc. There can also be a general reluctance to behave businesslike or professionally.

What does this negative behavior contribute? It contributes to obstacles to increased productivity, higher salaries, more jobs, advancement, and other work-related concerns and barriers. Effectively, we see growth and development stifled for the individual and the organization (or the country, as the case may be).

We can learn from citizens from underdeveloped countries who immigrate to developed nations. These same individuals with negative and obstructionist attitudes in their homelands have markedly different perspectives in their new homes. The opportunities provided by governments of developed countries help these individuals acquire positive attitudes (or, perhaps, shed the negativity they learned in their native land). As a result, these citizens work hard to succeed because their positive attitudes propel them to success.

If your organization is struggling, start evaluating at the top of the hierarchy to determine what leaders are doing to help their employees have a positive and productive mindset. Like opportunities in developed countries, positive attitudes and strong work ethics trickle down from the top.

Learning at Work

How is your workday going? What have you learned from your job and/or from your peers? If you aren't learning at work, how rewarding is your job? In addition to working to maintain a satisfactory standard of living, informal learning at work adds to an individual's work satisfaction.

Various reports hold that informal learning in the workplace accounts for about 90 percent of everything employees learn. This statistic may be accurate if we consider Albert Bandura's social learning theory, which posits that we learn through observing others' behaviors and attitudes and the outcomes of those behaviors.

Bandura[28] explains that there are four conditions for modeling behavior. These are:

- Attention. Different factors can increase or decrease one's attention to a particular behavior, such as the behavior's distinctiveness, its effect on your emotions (positive or negative emotions are more likely to be remembered than behavior that did not evoke an emotional response), prevalence and complexity of the behavior, and functional value (e.g., how important is the behavior to your job?). An individual's characteristics also affect attention to the behavior (e.g., sensory capacities, arousal level, perceptual set, past reinforcement, etc.).

- Retention. Remembering what you observed is retention. Symbolic coding[29] impacts retention, as do mental images, cognitive organization, symbolic rehearsal, and motor rehearsal (i.e., practicing what we observed).

- Reproduction. This condition relates to "doing" what we observed. It includes attention to our physical capabilities to reproduce the behavior, including feedback mechanisms through self-observation. How well are we producing the observed behavior?

- Motivation. To imitate behavior, we need to have a good reason to do so. This reason may include motivators such as history (e.g., perhaps past behaviors did not result in good outcomes, so we desire a new behavior), or it may involve promised or imagined incentives.

Like many social and cultural theorists, Bandura believed that the world and a person's behavior cause each other—we behave based on our environment and create an environment based on our behavior. Either way, organizations should take heed of the role that informal and social learning have in the workplace and encourage appropriate learning to maximize efficiency and performance. The following are five ways to increase informal learning in the workplace.

1. Mentoring. Coaching and mentoring help improve training and learning. Knowledge sharing is also a great way to retain knowledge in the workplace and prepare for succession.

2. Sharing. Social learning flourishes when people get into the habit of sharing their knowledge. Having a center of learning available on the corporate intranet or some other internal forum will go a long way to helping employees collaborate and boost their learning.

3. Experts. Provide expert resources for employees – knowing who to turn to when they have a question will go a long way to helping employees learn from each other.

4. Rewards. Some companies reward an employee's hard work with accolades such as "Employee of the Month" or "Top Contributor," making learning fun. Another way to make learning fun is through gamification – who doesn't love a good game of *Scrabble for Business*?

5. Mandatory learning. Ensuring that employees complete one level of learning before they can advance to the next level is an excellent way to ensure that they are reading the corporate handbook (so to speak). An online learning platform can readily provide this learning, ensuring collaboration and social learning become part of the employees' learning journey.

Would you like to know how you can learn better from work? Check out the Learning Innovations Laboratory report about the three stances that make a difference[30] at work: completion, performance, and development.

Motivating for Change

Conventional organizational change usually fails. That's because you and your employees look at things differently.

In traditional organizations, employers expect employees to do what they are told (i.e., their jobs for which they receive compensation). Some leaders still believe that motivating people to change involves telling or persuading them to change. This thinking stems from an early age of having expectations imposed on us—first by our parents and teachers and later by our employers.

But times have changed.

Today, we judge organizations on how well they meet corporate responsibility, fair trade, sustainability, and the triple bottom line (profit, people, and planet). The judging comes from all levels—customers, employees, and the public. Because people have this new perspective on their world, imposing change on people will not work. Here's why:

- Individual needs are not the same as those of the organization.

- Individuals lead busy lives (even outside of work), so they are not able or willing to assimilate change just because the organization says so.

Given these new paradigms, organizations that implement successful change can align their aims with the total life needs of their employees—that's why addressing WII-FM ("What's in it for me?") is so important. Leaders who know how to tap into each individual's WII-FM will build urgency and momentum for the change and make the change stick.

To help you with your change initiative, consider these facts:

1. People will never align with destructive aims. Reassess and realign your organization's vision and mission to ensure that it meets corporate responsibility, aims for the sustainability of the environment, favors fair trade, and is opposed to exploitation and executive greed, to name a few.

2. People cannot multi-task or learn new skills without some job realignment. The organization must consider several things, not the least of which are individual capacities for change (absorptive capacity). Consulting with employees to learn how they think change will impact their jobs helps to see change from both perspectives.

Ignoring the above facts is a sure guarantee of failed change initiatives. Consider also that at least 75 percent of the organization's leadership must buy into the change to succeed. This buy-in means that the organization's change leader must provide compelling evidence of the change to leaders *first* and staff *second*.

When at least 75 percent of the organization's leadership supports the change, selling the change to staff becomes much easier. Then, the potential for change to stick becomes a reality rather than a hope. In the bigger picture, hope is never a strategy.

Dimensions of Change

Are you and your organization productive and efficient? Most people say that they and their organization are both. However, I have found this not to be the case in many organizations.

At a recent process and value stream mapping exercise, staff wanted to improve their operations. They acknowledged that they had many process issues that needed fixing. However, they were confused about how they or the organization should proceed. They were also frustrated, indicating that their busy schedules would hamper change. This organization is not atypical in its reaction to change.

In managing organization-wide change, researchers have identified six elements that must be in place for the transition to succeed. If any of the elements is missing, successful change will not occur. Here is how these elements impact organizational change:

- If there is no vision, there is confusion.

- If there are insufficient skills, there is anxiety.

- If there are no incentives, there is resistance.

- If there are inadequate resources, there is frustration.

- If there is no action plan, there are false starts.

- If there is no collegiality, there is isolation.

When an organization has a vision, it focuses on achieving the vision. Whether through strategic, business, or service plans, the vision must be clear and communicated to all staff, who must understand the vision. The organization's goals and objectives are clear when staff understand the vision.

Sufficient skills to meet the organization's strategy are crucial to change. If skills are lacking, staff will feel anxious about their roles. When anxiety is present, inefficiency and poor productivity are also present. Provide training, coaching, and counseling to ensure staff have the necessary skills to do their jobs.

Incentives are significant for motivating staff to change. Financial and non-financial rewards can be equally effective at stimulating change. Examples of financial rewards include fair compensation, bonuses for work performance, relocation support, and housing. Non-financial incentives may consist of quality culture, public recognition, awards, study leave, and workplace mentoring, to name a few.

Resources are another critical factor in successful change. If there are insufficient resources to make change happen, then change will not occur or will be slow to emerge. Depending on the organization's desire for change, resources must be ample so that staff are not discouraged by the pace of change.

Sometimes, organizations forget about the importance of having action plans in place to guide change. An action (or implementation) plan provides everyone with a "road map" to change. In short, it allows all those involved in the change process to know what the organization expects, who is responsible, and the timeline and process for achieving tasks to effect change.

Also, don't forget about collegiality. It's much nicer to work with colleagues with whom you share mutual respect than to endure hostility. Organizations need to ensure that their staff are well suited to the culture and that the culture promotes collegiality.

Managing change is not an easy task, especially if the change involves a large-scale project, but if all of the dimensions of change are in place, successful change can be a certainty.

Head, Heart, Hands – Do You Know What You're Doing?

We all do it—incessantly discharge tasks so that we can move on to the next one. Sometimes, in our haste, we become overwhelmed with uncompleted work waiting for our attention, stopping us in our tracks. Why do we bother with completing task after task since there never seems to be a finish line? This "hum" of never-ending tasks usurps our energy and causes us to view work as an irritation rather than an opportunity.

When we find ourselves diverted from our work by the barrage of demands in our minds, it is because we have not understood the purpose of what we are doing. This lack of understanding occurs when we do not activate all three thinking centers, i.e., head, heart, and hands. We must work purposefully to reduce brain hum and accomplish tasks efficiently. Let me explain what I mean.

The head, heart, and hands framework balances what you know and feel, who you are, and what you do. In business, we instinctively gear to using information (head) to execute tasks without considering how this approach impacts our attitude/emotions (heart) or our actions (hands) toward our work. If we don't engage all three activation centers, we speed through tasks to get to the next one (i.e., think of robots). In the process, we become devoid of feelings toward our work, spiraling through it, hoping that the next task will be better once we complete this one. This approach reduces our efficiency and our productivity. It also increases our dissatisfaction with the work.

To become truly efficient and productive in everything we do, we must focus on our work with our heads, hearts, and hands. The more we can concentrate emotionally, the more we can productively engage with our work. As a result, our efficiency soars. One of the best ways to develop focus is by having fun with your work.

Have fun with your work by viewing it objectively (i.e., place it in your mind's "hand" to look at what you are to do and the purpose of the task). Do you understand what you're doing or the expectations of you on this task? You can successfully execute when you know what the work is about and how you feel about it.

Practice engaging with your work using the head, heart, and hands framework to understand what you wish to accomplish and to change your behavior toward your work. The resulting improved efficiency will create a happier you, quashing the endless hum of tasks and creating clarity of purpose.

Reclaiming Knowledge Work's Lost Productivity

In the mid-twentieth century, Peter Drucker coined the term "knowledge worker" and said that the knowledge worker's productivity would be the biggest twenty-first-century management challenge. He was right. Knowledge and manual workers are no longer exclusive—technology has blurred the lines of work such that even workers loading products onto conveyor belts are no longer exempt from being classified as knowledge workers.

Without technology and the onslaught of the need to process information, productivity was easier to measure (inputs and outputs) since the work was easier to see. In the typical factory setting, workers come to work, see the work in front of them, and finish it. One can see how much product the workers produce. But how does one measure the value of a report or meeting without a tangible product? Not only is knowledge work productivity more challenging to measure, but productivity has also decreased because of knowledge work.

One of the reasons for lowered productivity in knowledge work is the greater need for critical thinking skills, skills that were not in demand in the early twentieth century. These skills include the ability to make decisions about what we need to do with the paperwork on our desks, the ability to understand and monitor the outcomes and required actions to complete our tasks successfully, and the ability to follow a schedule that allows us the freedom to prioritize our work as suits our working style and our employer's requirements. Depending on whether we execute these skills efficiently determines whether we are productive.

In addition to the need for critical thinking skills and efficient execution of individual work plans, organizations can no longer selectively disseminate information to their workers if they expect to improve organizational productivity. They must share everything so all employees can glean what is helpful. For example, some companies share their day sales and inventory numbers with everybody in the company. Companies recognize that their employees will do better if they understand how their actions contribute to or detract from business results.

Improving an organization's productivity is no longer a selective process and cannot be done in silos. It must involve the entire organization. Here are five things you can do right now to improve your organization's productivity:

1. Share all company information. The organizations' executives can no longer hide information behind the "need to know." Everyone in the organization needs to know what's going on. If organizations keep people in the dark, your company limits productivity.

2. Eliminate deep hierarchical structures. They serve no one well in the organization, least of all those at the top.

3. Involve all employees in decision-making. It may be precisely the insights of the mail room clerk that can help your company move its strategic plan forward.

4. Use technology to improve information sharing and collaboration. Upgrade your records and information systems so that everyone can access information readily. Implement workflow systems to enable everyone to be more productive.

5. Use annual performance reviews to set individual goals and find out from each employee how well they think the company is doing. This meeting should be a time of joint goal setting and improvement for the coming year.

Productivity doesn't happen by itself. The thinking that goes into knowledge work can provide powerful outcomes for an organization.

However, this can only occur if the organization recognizes and supports the potential of its workers. It can be a productive win–win.

Good, Better, Best

Do you remember a time when you tried to do your very best on an exam or an assignment? What about preparing for a presentation at work or planning a meeting, or delivering a seminar? How did it feel? Do you remember how much effort you put in to do your best? If you did your very best, there is a strong likelihood that you also got the best reward for your efforts and were happy with the results.

Best is not the same as perfect. Being perfect carries the burden of unnecessary effort that does not reap an equivalent reward. Perfectionism involves setting impossible standards that have an impossible probability of being achieved. Best, on the other hand, is doing what you can do to a high standard that you can achieve. It means extending beyond average – going beyond good – to do your very best.

Doing your best is not the same as being the best. If you aim to be the best, you may end up with disappointments and impossibilities that are as difficult to achieve as if you are a perfectionist. Wanting to be the best at something is not a bad goal, but there must be a balance between winning (being the best) and losing (not being the best). For instance, if you enjoy sports, you know that only one team earns the label "the best" each season, even though all teams try to do their best.

When one does their best, they focus on the present to be as efficient and productive as possible, ensuring that the final product or service is of the highest quality. When you deliver high quality, you can take pride in your work because you expended the necessary effort to perform well, even if you did not qualify to be the best.

Contrast best with good or better. If you deliver a good product or service, knowing that you could have done better, how does this make you feel? There's that knowledge that you could have done better, right? Whatever you do, if you know you could have done better, you have not delivered your best results, which means you haven't provided your most efficient or productive work.

An interesting facet of doing your best at everything is that the lines between your work and personal life eventually get blurred. Over time, you start to love what you do, continually expending your best effort in whatever you do.

Focusing on the present to do your best frees you from superfluous thoughts that may impact your best performance. If you keep in the present to do your best, there will come a time when you won't be able to distinguish between work and play because both will be equally enjoyable. Ultimately, that is the best achievement in life.

Out with the Old, In with the New

A surprising fact is that most of us have *NO* difficulty accepting change. This acceptance is despite 80 percent of change initiatives failing the first time out of the gate. What's wrong with this picture, you ask?

It appears that the difficulty in implementing change is not accepting the idea. The challenge is in the sustained practice or application of the concept (or improvement initiative). In other words, the problem with our reaction to change does not relate to our ability to let new ideas in. The problem is in getting our old ideas out.

One of two things occurs with new ideas – you believe the new initiative is the best way, or you think your old way of doing the same thing is better. Simultaneously believing in both creates discord.

You can't have it both ways: Discord leads to failed change initiatives.

Successful organizations remove the discord and likely incorporate the practice of bio-psychology of change into their change projects. There is a difference between a rational approach to change management and a bio-psychological approach. Only the bio-psychological approach leads to successful change initiatives. Here is how it works.

1. Communicate the vision. Before change can occur, people need to be aware of potential changes. Working in small groups and with key individuals will go a long way to ensuring that the idea for the change initiative takes hold, priming people to listen.

2. Identify the area for change. Have individuals focus on the change and relate their thoughts, feelings, and experiences about their existing circumstances. In doing so, individuals can "see" that their circumstances require change.

3. Assessment and diagnosis. With the circumstances described, have the individual talk about their conflicting behaviors, feelings, and thoughts that may get in the way of accepting the change. What coping patterns are they using in the existing circumstances?

4. Plan the change. Once assessment and diagnosis are complete, ask the individual what behavior they can do less of (e.g., coping behaviors) to have room for this new behavior (new change initiative) in their

brain map space. Discuss their feelings relating to letting go of the old behavior.

5. Implement the change. Using pilot projects, implement the change incrementally or visualize the steps until you reach your goal. Repetition of incremental steps may be necessary until you achieve success.

6. Monitor the change, successes, and risks. Use coaching to help individuals stay on track with their new behavior, accept the change, and insert it as the behavior of choice in their brain map space.

Conducting regular check-ins after implementing change will help identify areas for further improvement. Early detection helps with the early correction of failures and continuing improvements.

CONTROL

Measures of Control

Several recent experiences forced me to the same conclusion: Organizations that place many controls on their processes do so because their operations are flawed in the first place. Let me give you an example.

A process mapping exercise with a service provider revealed the following:

- 37.3% of the steps in the process add value to the end product/customer

- 21.9% of the steps add no value to the process ("wastes")

- 40.8% of the steps add no value but appear necessary for some business or regulatory purpose ("necessary wastes")

The striking thing about this process is that most tasks (i.e., 40.8%) are business non-value adding (BNVA)—solely existing to manage the process. The problem with BNVA tasks is that they inhibit workflow in any organization, and the organization should minimize them. Less than one percent of process tasks are typically BNVA in an efficient organization. These BNVAs are necessary to comply with legislation.

However, organizations heavy with BNVA tasks include necessary tasks for regulatory purposes and impose upon themselves BNVA steps because they do not trust their processes or systems. The organization tries to overcome this lack of confidence by adding more controls to the processes or systems to make them more efficient. This approach exacerbates the problem.

The organization cannot eliminate genuine BNVA tasks, but it is good practice to reduce their cycle time by simplifying the process. In essence, BNVAs are part of the cost of doing business—customers don't see the BNVAs, but they pose a time and cost for the company. For example, completing forms for regulators or inspectors concerning products developed and shipped or services provided is a necessary cost of doing business.

Organizations should focus on eliminating the non-value-adding steps (wastes) and enhancing the value-adding steps (activities for which the customer is willing to pay) to improve business processes. The best way to do this is by measuring your process since you can only improve what you measure—i.e., let data/evidence be your guide.

Realistically, no organization can expect to be 100% productive all the time, but baseline data will provide the means to measure your continuous improvement implementation.

Continuously improving your processes will help you decrease control steps (BNVA) and eliminate non-value-adding steps (wastes). It will also provide more value-adding work the customer is willing to pay for and accept.

Only through a continuous improvement approach will your company be able to assure productivity gains in the long term. Also, a continuous improvement program will help free up time in your day so you can focus on more creative and strategic objectives to help you and your organization be even more productive and profitable.

What Keeps Leaders Awake?

In a recent Aon Global Risk Consulting risk management survey, organizations cited 50 concerns keeping them awake at night. The top three in 2021 were cyber attacks/data breaches, business interruption, and economic slowdown/slow recovery. The following two of the top five risks were commodity price risk/scarcity of materials and damage to reputation/brand.

While many organizations prepare for risk, focusing only on one organizational risk in today's interconnected world is challenging. Risks affecting one organization do not always isolate to just that organization. Corporations (and countries) can no longer function as islands or enjoy immunity from risks affecting others. Look at the economy, for instance.

In 2009, the problems in the small country of Greece did not remain solely within its borders. It disrupted markets worldwide, its problems spilling to Ireland, Portugal, Spain, Italy, Cyprus, and others. Even before the Greece crisis, the United States was dealing with its economic woes in 2008—many organizations felt its mortgage issues around the country and the globe. Then, there was the COVID-19 pandemic in 2020–2022; its repercussions interrupted every business.

On top of economic struggles and perhaps because of them, governments have taken on more power in regulating government and business. This regulation includes the financial sector and all industries. New and changing regulations are a risk for corporations—the need is to adapt processes quickly to ensure regulators are happy.

Competition can affect corporate brands, forcing big players to innovate and differentiate to survive the competitive onslaught. While survival is the stopgap, thriving is the goal.

Do you remember the "Super Size Me" documentaries? They forced McDonald's to offer healthier meal choices on its menu. It was a matter of brand reputation (which ranks fifth on Aon's 2021 list). As commentators dragged McDonald's through the documentaries, other fast food chains took note and followed quickly to update their menus. None wanted individuals to link their food/menu with obesity and poor health.

While most risks can be managed efficiently by organizations that proactively practice continuous improvement, those that scramble to react to crises are doomed to fall further behind. Think about business interruption, for example.

Major and natural disasters may impact whole communities, but smaller disasters can also wreak havoc, although we rarely hear about smaller disasters. What happens if your library's basement gets flooded? Do you have a contingency plan to salvage your information? Have you practiced the plan? What about if your computer system crashes? How will this impact your business?

If it occurs, business interruption does not need to happen for prolonged periods if the organization is ready to deal with anything. Lean organizations that practice efficiency in all processes are more agile in addressing small or large disasters. Bloated organizations can never be as ready to handle problems or quickly recover from disasters.

To be highly efficient and effective, here are four considerations:

1. Implement and maintain a continuous improvement strategy so that your organization can handle any risk at any time.

2. Ensure that organizational policies and procedures are current. Test them to make sure they make sense and enable productivity, especially in the face of risk.

3. Train and re-train all staff so they understand policies, procedures, and their

roles and responsibilities in the organization.

4. Develop an organization-wide culture that includes efficiency, effectiveness, and productivity. This culture starts with leaders championing the culture shift and then practicing the change. Lead by example.

Organizations that plan for the future by incorporating a continuous cycle of efficient and effective practices will thrive even when faced with adversity. Those that do not have a healthy risk management strategy may not survive.

Taming Insomnia to Improve Productivity

There are so many reasons to get a good night's sleep: you feel better, you look better, you perform better, and people like being around you. In short, sleep allows us to be our best selves. The benefits of quality sleep extend beyond feelings, ranging from reducing stress to improving productivity.

Most healthy adults need between seven and nine hours of sleep each night. When we lose even one hour of sleep, we experience fatigue the next day, and our ability to function may be as effective as an individual whose blood alcohol level is .08. Not sleeping enough also has other implications, including:

- Lack of motivation

- Moodiness and irritability

- Reduced creativity and problem-solving skills

- Reduced immunity

- Concentration and memory problems

- Overeating and weight gain

- Impaired motor skills and increased risk of accidents

- Difficulty making decisions

- Increased risk of diabetes, heart disease, and other health problems

What do you do if insomnia prevents you from dropping off right away? A study[31] found that sleep interventions such as constructive worry, imagery distraction, or gratitude effectively relieve insomnia. Here is how the techniques work.

1. Constructive worry. Set aside 15 minutes earlier in the day (before 8:00 p.m.) and write out worries and concerns that will likely interfere with sleep and steps toward their resolution. Then, if worry creeps in at bedtime, remind yourself that you already devoted time to these concerns and will do so again tomorrow when you are less tired and better able to think of good solutions.

2. Imagery distraction. This distraction involves closing your eyes and imagining an interesting, engaging, pleasant, and relaxing situation. For instance, imagine being on a holiday, a sunny beach, or a happy family occasion. This imagery will calm your mind, allowing you to drift to sleep.

3. Gratitude is another distraction technique. When one is under stress, it is common to be preoccupied with worries and concerns and to ignore the positive experiences in one's life. Shifting your attention to what you are grateful for (i.e., all the positive events in your life) distracts you from worry. Focusing on the positives lifts your mood and allows you to fall asleep more easily.

If you are sleep-deprived, try one or all of the above techniques to help you get and stay asleep so you can wake up refreshed.

Finally, remember to schedule enough time for sleep every day by making sleep a top priority on your to-do list.

Secret to Enabling a Paradigm Shift

Do you have a paradigm? Yes, of course; we all do. We use paradigms as a frame of reference for whatever we do. Paradigms are the boundaries that tell us what to do to succeed within those boundaries. Imagine the following thoughts and how they can limit success.

In the early 1900s, when silent movies were the rage, some people thought no one would ever want to hear actors talk.

In the early 1900s, at the dawn of computer invention, a particular CEO thought that the world market would only want about five computers. At the same time, another high-ranking executive indicated there would never be a need for individuals to have computers in their homes.

As you can see, paradigms can be huge inhibitors to success. To enable continuous improvement in our organizations, we need people to shift their paradigms. We can do this by engaging people to work together to see/feel the impact of improvements. Let me show you what I mean.

Let's say you want your organization to decrease waste. First, create a team that will lead the change on your behalf. Then, invite the team to a Kaizen event and set the stage for the paradigm shift by encouraging people to get to know each other, really get to know each other. By building mutual respect among team members, you are enabling people to shift their paradigms (i.e., those with mutual respect are more open to listening to and accepting new ideas from others).

Another critical aspect of enabling paradigm shifts is engaging people to see where improvements are needed. For example, during Kaizen events, people go into the workplace to find examples of waste in each of the eight categories (defects, overproduction, waiting, non-utilized talent, transportation, inventory, motion, and extra-processing). This exercise alone is an eye-opener for many; their excitement in seeing the waste firsthand ignites their enthusiasm for eliminating waste. In addition, having groups see the wastes by developing value stream maps of the processes solidifies their resolve to improve the situation.

Do you see how we get people to change their paradigms? By teaching about waste and Lean (in this instance) and allowing people to apply their knowledge by physically searching for each of the eight wastes in their workplace, they experience the waste. Then, they look at the wastes in the overall process using value stream maps while interacting and building mutual respect for other team members. There is no better feeling than seeing the shift in thinking from "We've always done it this way, and it can't be done differently" to "Wow, look at all the things we can improve to make the process even better."

With the most significant hurdle now overcome (paradigm shift), all you need to do is maintain the momentum for continuous improvement in your organization.

Moving to a Quality Culture

Look at your organization. Is it just good enough? Moving to a quality culture is crucial to stand out from the crowd. This shift means listening to customers and continuously improving operations.

The definition of culture is the combined/shared values and beliefs of a group of people. Their values and beliefs are their internal motivators, which manifest in their behaviors. Thus, an organization demonstrates its culture through its employees' behaviors. For example, an organization that believes in consistency, fairness, communication, and team involvement would display behaviors of productivity, quality, enhanced group morale, and individual satisfaction.

Thus, a quality culture's characteristics include a competitive environment where employees continually raise their work quality to outperform peers. It also consists of a culture of being friendly to customers and fellow employees and challenging design assumptions.

How does one move to a quality culture? It does so by moving from a victim mindset (i.e., blaming employees for what goes wrong in the organization) to being a leader and having a player mindset (i.e., questioning your responses to a situation to see if you could have handled things differently, without blaming others). A quality culture includes values and beliefs that drive quality behaviors. Once an organization's values and beliefs change, so do employee behaviors.

How does one change their behaviors to emulate a quality culture? Here are a few things you can do.

1. Grow through adversity. When things are difficult, ask what worked and what didn't. Could you have done something differently? What can you learn for the future?

2. Build strength through frustration. Don't give up if things don't work out the way you planned the first time. Evaluate the situation and determine how to do things differently next time.

3. Role model leadership behaviors. Leaders are responsible for the environment of their employees. Create space that enables team members to become players/leaders.

4. Grow through challenge and support. Ensure the team has a good mix of challenge and support to understand their responsibilities and that their success depends on each team member.

5. No blame, no judging. A quality culture does not blame or judge people. It involves evaluating the process to learn what could have been done better or differently. What worked? What didn't? How can we improve the process so the situation doesn't repeat?

6. Responsibility. In a quality culture, everyone takes some responsibility for the process. When each person does their bit, the process should flow smoothly. Be open-minded. Share information before it's needed. Take the initiative. Learn from mistakes. Give credit when due.

You may have heard that life is 10 percent what happens to us but 90 percent how we react. Thus, failures are only failures if we fail to learn from our mistakes. Ultimately, the people are the only difference between a quality culture and an organization without a quality culture. The greater the interactions of the organization's people, the greater the organization's value.

To build a quality culture, practice value-added behaviors such as humility, calmness, compassion, listening, reflection, honesty, patience, humor, discipline, etc. Remember that problems are not things; they are merely assessments of things. We have a choice of how to react to a problem. Choose to be a player and fully participate in the choice to respond to the problem as a problem or become part of the solution to the problem.

Choose to be a player to build a quality culture. Be the solution.

Efficiency is in the Toolkit

Social media, instant messaging, and other similar information-sharing mechanisms contribute to an ever-increasing overload of demands for more–better–faster. Unfortunately, this information overload isn't going away; it will only increase. So, while tools help us navigate the ever-increasing complexity of our work, organizations need to catch up.

Organizations, be it public or private enterprises, typically implement infrastructures, tools, and processes that make it easier for the organization but not necessarily easy for the individual. This approach is because most organizations don't think down to the level of the individual doing the work.

In fairness, many productivity tools in older, well-established companies worked well at the beginning many years ago. However, to sustain and improve productivity, organizations need to re-examine the tasks required to complete a job and then work backward to determine what tools would be the most efficient.

Here are six considerations for improving employee productivity in a technologically fast-paced work environment.[32]

1. Clarity. Be clear when sharing information with your staff. Communicating requirements allows employees to work smarter and faster. Clear communication creates efficiency and productivity in the workplace.

2. Navigation. Employees must quickly navigate and find whatever they need to complete their tasks. When information is easy to find, efficiency and productivity increase.

3. Basics. Getting the right information in the right way and the right amount is a basic tenet of efficiency. If basics are not available in your organization, the organization wastes time.

4. Usability. Ensure that corporate-built stuff is easy to use. Sometimes, out-of-the-box products far outweigh the time and effort organizations spend to custom build. For instance, it's not usable if it takes seven hours to print a report or fifteen minutes to load a program.

5. Speed. Products, tools, and information—anything employees use to do their job—must be fast enough to do it efficiently. If speed is slow, employees experience wasted time, efficiency, and productivity.

6. Time. Employers must respect their employees' time and use it wisely and

effectively. Don't waste your employees' time, and they won't waste yours.

Ideally, organizations should examine management tools (e.g., strategic plans), work tools (e.g., software), and collaboration and learning tools (e.g., company intranet) from the employees' perspective. For example, do your employees understand the organization's strategic plan or budgeting and reporting documents? Are your databases and laptops enabling or hindering work productivity? Is your intranet an easy-to-navigate learning tool?

These and other considerations, when perfected, will do more to earn your employees' respect than any monetary rewards. Change your working environment to include a holistic view of employees' needs to help them do their best. When you do, your organization's productivity improves, and so do its profits.

Open Office – Productivity Enabler or Slasher?

In 2014, about 70 percent of employees in the United States worked in open offices. Despite this high number, you may be surprised to learn that the open office concept is not the be-all and end-all for everyone. Success depends on personal work styles and personalities and how well workers can adapt to the high distraction level served by open offices. For example, in 2019, the Harvard Business Review reported that when firms switched to open offices, face-to-face interactions fell by 70 percent, while electronic interactions increased to compensate.[33]

In addition, a few studies[34] found that workers in open-plan offices get sick more often (62 percent more sick days on average), they don't like the noise (sound and temperature are the most critical factors in the environment), older workers *really* don't like the noise (those over 45 are more sensitive to noise and temperature), and open offices deplete productivity.

The most significant impact on productivity tends to be distractions such as overhearing conversations, ringing phones, and noisy machines. In addition, employees experience decreased job satisfaction and lower perceived privacy as factors negatively affecting productivity. Another interesting finding is that workers in open offices are more stressed and less satisfied with their work environment, resulting in a breakdown of team relationships.

Perhaps not surprisingly, the noise in open offices decreases cognitive performance. In addition, open office commotion impairs workers' ability to recall information and do basic arithmetic.[35] Listening to music to block out office intrusion does not help; even that impairs mental acuity.

While open offices seem to be better suited to younger workers, a study in 2012[36] found that certain types of noise, such as conversations and laughter, are equally distracting to Generation Y workers and their older counterparts. However, younger workers enjoyed the camaraderie of open spaces, valuing their time spent socializing with coworkers. While younger workers acknowledge the problems of open offices, they see them as fair trade-offs for the greater good. But the trade is not as great as it might seem.

Regardless of age, when we experience too many inputs at once – a computer screen, conversation, music, telephones, email alerts – our senses become overloaded, and we must exert more effort to achieve the desired result. Those unable to screen out distractions in the office are frantic multitaskers.

Thus, the multitasking millennial seems more open to distraction. However, their wholehearted embrace of open offices may be ingraining a cycle of underperformance in their generation: They enjoy, build, and proselytize for open offices but may suffer the most from them in the long run.

The tried and true traditional offices that include cubicles are still the best despite their drawbacks. Research leads us to believe that employees are far more productive (and happier) in these controlled and focus-driven environments than in the open office.

Nonetheless, the pandemic caused a significant shift in open and traditional offices. Despite many clinging to the open office plan regardless of the productivity disasters, most office work can and is done productively or more productively from home. Whether these workers are more productive because they are working from home or whether it is because they are away from the open floor plan is another question.

The solution is quite simple, given the considerable pushback of employees not wanting to return to the office post-pandemic. If organizations want employees to return to the central office, they must provide workers with a more desirable workplace than the home offices that employees currently prefer.

Leaders Helping Staff with Productivity

In the world of high-octane business, productive leaders set the pace. But what about their staff? How can leaders help their staff be more productive? The short answer to this is through empowerment. Empowered staff are more productive and contribute more to the business and the bottom line.

If you think employee empowerment is not necessary for productivity, think again. Several case studies paint a compelling picture of empowerment. For example, in one study of account executives in a U.S. specialty mortgage banking company, actively disengaged account executives produced 28% less revenue than their engaged colleagues. Further, those not engaged generated 23% less revenue than their engaged counterparts. In this case, the statistics showed that employee engagement did not merely correlate with bottom-line results; it *drove* the results.

In addition, employee empowerment or engagement affects the mindset of people. Engaged employees *believe* they can make a difference in the organizations for which they work. Consider the following statistics to support this statement:

- 84% of highly engaged employees believe they can positively impact the quality of their organization's products, compared with only 31% of the disengaged

- 72% of highly engaged employees believe they can positively affect customer service, compared to 27% of the disengaged

- 68% of highly engaged employees believe they can positively impact costs in their job or unit, compared with 19% of disengaged employees.

However, research[37] of more than 600 U.S. businesses with 50–500 employees shows that 63.3% of companies say retaining employees is more challenging than hiring them. Given this data, you can see that employee empowerment is critical for organizational success.

So, how does a leader go about empowering or engaging their staff? Here are six things that I find work well in any organization.

1. Talk to your staff. Let the staff know what it is that you are trying to achieve. That is, explain the company's vision and mission. Use plain, straightforward language that everyone can understand. When staff know what goals you are trying to achieve, they will align their work to achieve your goals.

2. Provide staff with necessary training. Remember that it costs more to replace staff

than it does to train existing staff. For instance, replacing a low-skilled hourly worker costs approximately half of the worker's annual salary. As skill levels and positions increase, so does the replacement cost. A C-level executive can cost three to five times the position's annual salary.

3. Delegate. Delegate work to your staff and encourage them to do their very best. Assist as required.

4. Free your staff. Free your staff not to think that they have to consult with you before they do even the smallest tasks.

5. Don't hover. Set goals and priorities, and let your staff take responsibility for their tasks. This approach will stimulate them to succeed.

6. Reward your staff for their productivity. This reward can be through a verbal "great job" whenever appropriate and through money (always appreciated), such as bonuses or gift cards.

Moreover, evidence suggests that productive workers are likelier to be happy since productivity leads to job satisfaction. So, by empowering your staff, you are doing a good thing for the organization and its bottom line. You are also creating a happier workforce. Who wouldn't want to work with a happy workforce? I'm sure we all would.

Six Steps for Achieving Quality

We all intuitively understand quality. It's something that makes us appreciate a product or service, but describing that "something" can be difficult. From a customer's perspective, the customer is willing to pay for quality. From the organization's perspective, quality relates to a product's or service's conformance to specifications. These specifications are not only according to what the organization prescribes, but they also relate to the customer's expectations.

Ultimately, organizations that spend money on achieving quality systems and programs are more profitable than those that do not. This difference is because quality management programs prevent poor-quality products or services from reaching the customer. In addition, continuously improving existing quality practices ensures that the organization correctly develops products and services the first time.

Here are six steps to help you or your organization produce a quality product or service.

1. Define the quality characteristics of the product or service. These characteristics will be different for every type of product or service, depending on the industry. For

instance, you may be evaluating functionality (how well the product or service does its job), appearance (sensory characteristics), reliability (consistency of performance), durability, or some other quality.

2. Decide how to measure each quality characteristic. Depending on the quality characteristics, how will you measure functionality, for example, a restaurant, airline, bank, or computer? What characteristics of appearance are quality? What about reliability? And so on.

3. Set quality standards for each quality characteristic. This standard is the level of quality that defines the boundary between acceptable and unacceptable. Setting these standards can be challenging. For example, if one restaurant customer out of every 1,000 complains about the food, does that mean the other 999 are satisfied and, therefore, quality is good? Or are there other equally unhappy customers who did not complain? If this complaint level is similar for other restaurants, do we regard this as satisfactory quality?

4. Control quality against those standards. When setting standards, the organization must check its product's or service's conformance. This checking means product

or service delivery is done right the first time every time. As part of this control, the organization must decide where checks should occur, whether they should check every product or service (or should checking be confined to sampling), and how to perform the inspections.

5. Find and correct causes of poor quality. Implement total quality management tools and techniques to find and correct poor quality.

6. Continue to make improvements. As with Step 5 above, total quality management tools and techniques will help the organization cut its costs of poor quality and improve overall quality.

Remember to include employees in all quality improvement initiatives as your organization implements quality programs. If your employees are unhappy, there is a strong likelihood that your customers are also unhappy (even if customers are not complaining – see note under Step 3 above).

Consider this fact: About 68 percent of customers will stop doing business if they perceive an attitude of indifference from your staff. However, only 14 percent will leave if they are dissatisfied with your product or service, while nine percent leave for competitive reasons.

Include your employees in all quality programs for a healthy work environment and bottom line.

Procedures Par Excellence

Did you ever work for an employer where you received no documentation relating to the job's role and responsibilities when you arrived for work on your first day? I did. On my first day on the job, my instructions were to take it easy the first few days and deal with the work as it arose. Relying on the job description and job title for guidance, I performed my role as best I could and managed to stay with the company for two years. Perhaps no surprise, the company went out of business a few years after I left.

One cannot overstate the benefits of documented procedures. Among their many benefits, procedures make training of new employees easier. New employees invent the job's approaches when they do not have job guidelines. Then, when that employee leaves, the next employee reinvents or layers their invention on top of the pre-existing process. This approach leads to inefficiencies.

In addition to training, procedures provide a baseline for all continuous improvement activities in the organization. If you want to improve a specific process, how do you know what to improve if you can't specifically identify how the process should have been (or was) done in the first place?

Procedures help document standardized work. Organizations that have and use procedures are ahead of those that don't. If your organization does not have written guidelines, there is a 100 percent probability that your organization is inefficient. No procedures? Then, it's no surprise that your staff struggles with the how-to whenever they face a new customer request.

As well as a baseline for continuous improvement and standardizing work, procedures enable problem-solving. If an error occurs in a process, procedures allow you to pinpoint precisely where the error occurred and then correct that procedure so the problem does not reoccur. You won't need to fix the process on the fly or wing it.

Another benefit of procedures is the freedom they allow management not to micromanage. When management knows that standard operating procedures are in place for work processes, they do not need to stand over their employees' shoulders watching how they perform the work. Instead, they can focus on developing and working on the company's strategic vision while knowing that standard operations will get done consistently and effectively.

That's all great, you say, but your company already has procedures, and problems still occur. Remember that procedures are living documents, and organizations must update them occasionally. Look for tell-tale signs such as an increase in your company's accidents, higher failure rates, and costly returns, or if employees question normal operations and the company experiences a higher incidence of employee sick leave due to stress and overwhelm. Notice also the reasons for your customers' complaints. These situations may indicate that your procedures are due for a refresh.

Don't forget: The most effective procedures are those developed by the people doing the work, i.e., the subject matter experts. They don't necessarily have to write the guidelines, but they certainly have to provide input.

Efficiency Overload

Is there such a thing as too much efficiency? The short answer is "yes," but let me explain.

The goal of efficiency is to cut out waste and try to do more with less; the result is that the organization and the individuals in it are more effective (doing the right things – "quality") by being more efficient (doing things right – "productivity"). To achieve this goal, balancing efficiency with available organizational resources is necessary to ensure the correct amount of efficiency. It's really about getting the right balance.

If an organization does not have a precise balance of efficiency in its administrative and operational systems and processes, the resulting ineffectiveness may be worse than poor efficiency. For instance, asking employees to be efficient by measuring everything they do can cause operational paralysis. Employees cannot and should not reduce every task to numbers (e.g., How many emails did you answer today? Is your inbox at zero by the end of each day?). Instead, quality needs to be built into each task to enable efficiency through the resulting effectiveness.

Instead of "How many emails did you answer today," the question might be, "How many emails did you answer today that needed an answer today?"

Organizations and employees may disagree on whether there can be too much efficiency. The fact is that organizations need to continue to increase efficiencies to improve their competitiveness in the marketplace (or, in the case of non-profit or government organizations, to improve their service levels). Sometimes, this means layoffs and no raises—not favorable to employees. Without competitive advantage, however, organizations disappear, and in the process, all (not just some) of their employees lose their jobs. This scenario is why it is essential to implement the right balance of efficiency and effectiveness.

While efficiency may be easy to implement in an industrial or mechanical operation, effectiveness is more important than efficiency for knowledge workers. Everyone needs to become efficient using good time and process management principles. Applying efficiency techniques to tasks such as managing one's inbox, email, telephone calls, interruptions, etc., in a way that produces appropriate and quality results will enable knowledge workers to become more efficient and effective.

Implementing efficiency measures from the bottom up will ensure that each individual applies the appropriate balance to their work. This approach may help reduce the organization's zeal to implement mass efficiency measures that may not be appropriate for every employee.

Bridging the Gap between Training and Proficiency

Now that your staff has completed training in your organization's newest program, everyone knows what to do and how to do it. This expectation is reasonable, but the reality is that training does not mean that learning has occurred. Even less so, there is no guarantee of proficiency.

However, there are some ways to make ideas "stickier." They include ensuring simplicity, unexpectedness, concreteness, credibility, emotions, and stories.[38] These guidelines for making ideas stick are applicable in various situations, from selling to teaching. While these methods can make learning stick, they can also go a long way to enabling proficiency.

Research shows that retention of learning varies by modality. For instance, our retention is:

- 10 percent through reading
- 20 percent through hearing
- 30 percent through seeing
- 50 percent through hearing and seeing

- 70 percent through repeating the material (saying)

- 90 percent through saying and doing.

The above demonstrates that the more involved the learner is in the training, the higher the retention and the greater the likelihood of higher proficiency.

1. Make training simple. Training should be logical and not complicated. Short bursts of training are more effective than lengthy modules.

2. Introduce the unexpected into training. If the training concerns records management, stage a short play introducing real-life work scenarios about handling information. Sing a song about libraries or show a video about e-mail. Get creative and introduce the unexpected.

3. Make training concrete. Ensure that training demonstrates specific behaviors and steps, allowing learners to practice the behaviors and steps during and after training.

4. The trainer and training need to be credible. Learners need to trust the source to take the material seriously. The trainer's body language affects the learners' perception of credibility by 55 percent; voice accounts for

another 38 percent, but what the trainer says accounts for only seven percent. Pay attention to your body language.

5. Make training emotional. The best way to do this is to let learners know "what's in it for them" (i.e., WII-FM: what's in it for me). Learning the material may mean an increase in pay or a promotion at work. Nothing is more powerful than an emotional connection between the learner and the training to ensure that learning sticks.

6. Tell stories. Stories provide examples. People can relate to stories and are more apt to remember them than the training material.

Using the above techniques can help training stick, but pairing learners with coaches or mentors helps reinforce learning so that learners become proficient as they practice their knowledge.

Also, don't forget to audit learning at one month, three months, and nine months. Follow up post-training with learners to discuss if they require further information. It is through follow-up that training reinforcement occurs, allowing quick resolution of any issues that may arise.

About the Author

Mary Čolak has authored several newsletters and blogs on business, contentious issues, and life. *Lean Productivity and Efficiency* is her third book in the *Beyond Success* series. Her first and second books are *Considerations in Making Money* and *Acquiring Time*.

For over 30 years, Mary used her unique ability to turn chaos into order for organizations and individuals. She helps clients identify necessary organizational and personal work methods and systems improvements. As a result of her involvement, clients experience marked improvements in efficiency, productivity, and a reduction in their stress. In addition to working with organizations to improve business processes, Mary coaches individuals to help them manage and overcome obstacles in their job performance. Mary also taught operations management for seven years as a university instructor in a Bachelor of Business Administration program.

Mary is a lifelong learner. She has a Master of Arts degree in professional communication, a Bachelor of Arts in Psychology (major) and English (minor), and an Associate of Arts diploma in public administration. In addition, she has a master's certificate in Lean Six Sigma and was certified as a management consultant in 2004. Her awards and recognitions include the Outstanding Graduate award from the Institute of Public Administrators of Canada and an honors certificate from the Canadian Association of Management Consultants for getting the top mark in British Columbia on the comprehensive national management consulting case study examination.

Mary was born in Croatia and emigrated to Canada with her parents at a very young age. Today, she loves spending summers in her native Croatia but is happy to call Canada her home, where she lives and enjoys her life with her husband, children, and grandchildren.

Endnotes

---

[1] Undercover Boss is a reality television series first aired on British Channel 4 in 2009. The show was created by Stephen Lambert and produced in many countries. The show's format features a senior executive working undercover in their company to experience how their firm actually works and identifies areas for improvement. In addition, the executive's interaction with their staff usually ends up with them rewarding their hard-working employees.

[2] A Gantt chart is a visual project management tool used to plan, schedule, and track tasks and activities over a specific time. It is a graphical representation of a project's timeline, showing when tasks start and finish, and their dependencies. Henry L. Gantt, an American engineer and management consultant, developed this technique in the early twentieth century. A typical Gantt chart consists of horizontal bars, each representing a task or activity, arranged along a timeline. The length of each bar represents the duration of the task, and the bars are positioned on the chart based on their start and end dates. The Gantt chart can help stakeholders understand the project's progress, identify potential bottlenecks, and make informed decisions about resource allocation and scheduling adjustments. While Gantt charts are effective for many types of projects, more complex projects might require specialized project management software that offers additional features and customization options.

[3] Wansink, B., Painter, J. E., & North, J. (2005). Bottomless bowls: Why visual cues of portion size may influence intake. *Obestity Research 13*(1), 93–100.

[4] Eliyahu M. Goldratt developed the Theory of Constraints (TOC). The theory is a management philosophy and methodology focusing on improving organizational performance by identifying and addressing constraints, or bottlenecks, that limit an organization's ability to achieve

its goals. TOC provides a systematic approach to problem-solving and decision-making, with the ultimate goal of optimizing the flow of resources and achieving better results. TOC is applicable to a wide range of industries and sectors, from manufacturing to services to project management. It offers a holistic and systems-oriented approach to problem-solving, emphasizing the interconnectedness of various components within an organization.

[5] Alex Osborn's 1948 book, *Your Creative Power* is a classic exploration of creativity and generating ideas. The book is now in the public domain. Despite being written almost 80 years ago, the book's techniques and examples are still useful and relevant today: simply replace the names of today's businesses in the book to tell similar stories. According to Osborn, there are two types of thinking: judicial and creative. Judicial or logical thinking is a screening process, passing judgment on ideas. This type of thinking dominates the executive suites of most companies. On the other hand, creative thinking is a free flow. It's best for generating ideas with no screening until after one compiles all possible ideas. One of the surprising discoveries that Osborn recounted is that ideas don't just come from executives. Researchers were surprised that shop floor workers and farmers were more creative and generated more valuable creative ideas than most executives.

[6] Taylor, D. W., Berry, P. C., & Block, C. H. (1958). Does group participation when using brainstorming facilitate or inhibit creative thinking? *Administrative Science Quarterly, 3*(1), 23–47.
https://doi.org/10.2307/2390603.
https://www.jstor.org/stable/2390603

[7] Lehrer, J. (2012). Groupthink: The brainstorming myth. *Annals of Ideas*, January 30, 2012.

[8] Nemeth, C. J., Personnaz, M., Personnaz, B., & Goncalo, J. A. (2003). The liberating role of conflict in group creativity: A cross-cultural study. *IRLE Working*

Paper No. 90-03. http://irle.berkeley.edu/work-ingpapers/90-03.pdf

[9] *Learning to See* introduced the term "value stream" to our everyday vernacular. The book provides a standard symbolic language and framework allowing improved communication and sharing of process flow maps. A value stream map provides managers and executives a picture of the entire production process, including value and non-value-adding activities. Value stream mapping establishes a direction for the company. The book contains a case study for a fictional Acme Stamping company and takes you through the steps of mapping the current state of the value stream, looking for all the sources of waste. After identifying the waste, you draw a map of a leaner future and a value stream plan to guide implementation. Ultimately, the book makes complicated concepts simple.

[10] Krafcik, J. F. (1988). Triumph of the Lean production system. *Sloan Management Review, 30*(1), 40–52.

[11] Womack, J. P., & Jones, D. T. (1996). *Lean thinking: Banish waste and create wealth in your corporation.* London: Simon & Schuster.

[12] David, V. (2022 April 4). The 20 biggest companies in the world. *CareerAddict.* Accessed on May 5, 2023, from https://www.careeraddict.com/biggest-companies.

[13] Gartner, Inc. (2020, March 31). Gartner says growth companies are more actively collecting customer experience data than nongrowth companies. *Gartner Press Release.* Stamford, CI. Retrieved from https://www.gartner.com/en/newsroom/press-re-leases/2020-03-31-gartner-says-growth-companies-are-more-actively-collecting-customer-experience-data-than-nongrowth-companies

[14] Morrel–Samuels, P. (2002). *Getting the truth into workplace surveys.* Harvard Business Review.

[15] Pecoraro, J. (2012). Survey fatigue. *Quality Progress, 45*(10), 87.

[16] Jensen, B. (2000). *Simplicity*. Profile Books. ISBN 9781861975485.

[17] Cision (2011, June 13). *Study: Office Depot and SierraTradingPost.com rank first for fastest phone and email customer support among top 100 online retailers*. Retrieved May 9, 2023, from https://www.prweb.com/releases/2011/6/prweb8568043.htm.

[18] Evans, J. R., & Lindsay, W. M. (2004). *Management and control of quality*. South-western College Pub. ISBN 978-0324202236.

[19] Fiume, O. J., & Cunningham, J. (2003). *Real numbers: Management accounting in a Lean organization*. Managing Times Press. ISBN 978-0972809900.

[20] Rattner, N., & Prang, A. (2022, July 27). The worst flight delays at the world's busiest airports. *New York Times*. https://www.wsj.com/articles/the-worst-flight-delays-at-the-worlds-busiest-airports-see-the-list-11658889826

[21] Martin, H. (2022, July 22). Who is to blame for the summer of flight delays and cancellations? *Los Angeles Times*. https://www.latimes.com/business/story/2022-07-22/flight-delays-cancelations-summer-2022

[22] Harris, S. (2022, July 29). Toronto's Pearson airport has a PR problem: It's known as the worst airport in the world. *CBC News*. https://www.cbc.ca/news/business/toronto-pearson-airport-delays-1.6534360

[23] CTV News. (2022, June 9). *How delays at Pearson Airport got so bad: Aviation experts weigh in*. https://www.ctvnews.ca/canada/how-delays-at-pearson-airport-got-so-bad-aviation-experts-weigh-in-1.5940198

[24] Robert Maurer's book talks about the art of making great and lasting change through small, steady steps

(thus, "the Kaizen way"). Of note is that Kaizen is capable of circumventing the brain's built-in resistance to new behaviors. Ultimately, small rewards lead to big returns.

[25] See the Project Management Institute (pmi.org) for more information on project management including books and resources and certification.

[26] The planning phase of a project covers these nine project areas: project scope management, project schedule management, project cost management, project quality management, project resource management, project communication management, project risk management, project procurement management, and project stakeholder management. The tenth knowledge area (really, the first) is project integration management. For more information on all these knowledge areas, check ou the Project Management Institute's website and the Project Management Body of Knowledge.

[27] Dee Ward Hock (March 21, 1929 – July 16, 2022) was the founder and CEO of the Visa credit card association.

[28] Bandura, A. (1976). *Social learning theory*. Pearson. ISBN 978-0138167448.

[29] Symbolic coding constructs internal models of the environment that guide the person's future behavior. Cognitive guidance explains how the person should act in a specific situation. For example, in symbolic modeling, the learner imitates behaviors displayed by characters in books, plays, movies, or television and then "codes" those behaviors into their mind for imitation in real life. Thus, people might dress like television characters or act bravely like superheroes.

[30] Perkins, D., Rigolizzo, M., & Biller, M. (2013). *Learning better from work: Three stances that make a difference*. Learning Innovations Laboratory at Harvard Graduate School of Education.

[31] Digdon, N. & Koble, A. (2011). Effects of constructive worry, imagery distraction, and gratitude interventions on sleep quality: A pilot trial. *Applied Psychology: Health and Wellbeing, 3*(2), 193–260.

[32] Jensen, B. (2001). *Simplicity: The new competitive advantage in a world of more, better, faster.* Perseus Press. ISBN: 9780738204307.

[33] Bernstein, E., & Waber, B. (2019 November-December). *The truth about open offices.* Harvard Business Review.

[34] Richardson, A., Potter, J., Paterson, M., Harding, T., Tyler–Merrick, G., Kirk, R., Reid, K., & McChesney, J. (2017). Office design and health: A systematic review. *New Zealand Medical Journal, 130*(1467), 39–49. PMID: 29240739

[35] Mulligan, A. (2023). *How does noise affect workplace productivity?* Health and Medicine. Psychreg.

[36] Rasila, H., & Rothe, P. (2012). A problem is a problem is a benefit? Generation Y perceptions of open-plan offices. *Property Management, 30*(4), 362–375.

[37] Spender, J. (2020, July 8). *Research: Employee retention a bigger problem than hiring for small business.* Zenefits.com.

[38] Heath, C., & Heath, D. (2010). *Switch: How to change things when change is hard.* Crown Business.

Printed in the USA
CPSIA information can be obtained
at www.ICGtesting.com
JSHW020827200124
55354JS00004B/149